Greetings from

INDIANA

Steel Mills

DUNES

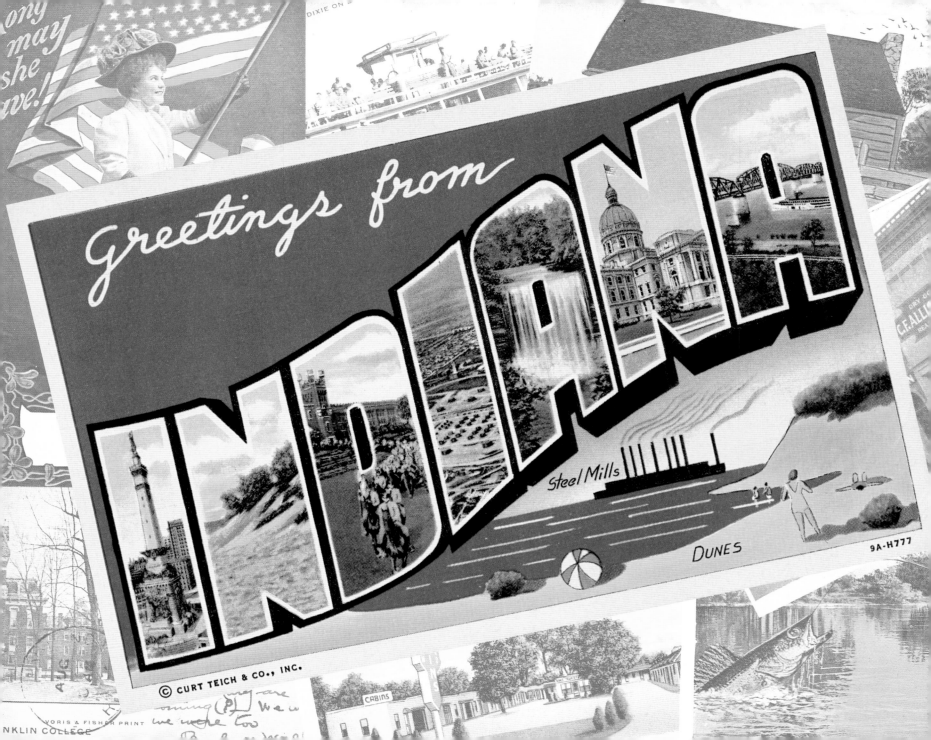

Vintage Hoosier Postcards

Robert Reed

INDIANA
University Press

Bloomington & Indianapolis

This book is a publication of

Indiana University Press
601 North Morton Street
Bloomington, IN 47404-3797 USA

http://iupress.indiana.edu

Telephone orders   800-842-6796
Fax orders   812-855-7931
Orders by e-mail   iuporder@indiana.edu

**Library of Congress Cataloging-in-
Publication Data**

Reed, Robert, date
  Greetings from Indiana : vintage Hoosier
postcards / Robert Reed.
     p. cm.
Includes bibliographical references.
  ISBN 0-253-21651-6 (alk. paper)
  1. Indiana—History—20th century—
Pictorial works.
2. Indiana—Social life and customs—20th
century—Pictorial works. 3. Indiana—
History, Local—Pictorial works. 4.
Historic sites—Indiana—Pictorial works.
5. Postcards—Indiana. I. Title.
  F527.R44 2003
  977.2'0022'2—dc21
                              2003008460

1 2 3 4 5 08 07 06 05 04 03

*Publication of this book has been
supported in part by The John Gallman
Fund for New Directions.*

This book is dedicated to my sister
Mary Lee Reed Druding
who still fondly remembers
the old log jail playground in
Nashville, Indiana.

Memory remains the gravity of all things past.

ony may she ve!

Greetings from

Bono, Ind.

DIXIE ON L

Abraham Lincoln's Boyhood

RUSHVILLE
301
LINE

C.F. ALLISC
DRY-GO
READ

SOUTH SIDE INN
FURNITURE
TOFT & SON

South

CABINS

My dear Nora:-
ibly come th
ut well be a
Friday mor
leet mid t
gage his ro
Eda & Mary,
th be there
be. Mary H
coming sure
M-C-7
Ede & Mary are
coming (P.) We w
we were too

VORIS & FISHER PRINT
NKLIN COLLEGE

Contents

Preface   ix

Acknowledgments   xi

Introduction   xiii

ONE •➤ *Alexandria to Brazil* ➤• 1

TWO •➤ *Camp Atterbury to Dyer* ➤• 11

THREE •➤ *Elkhart to French Lick* ➤• 25

FOUR •➤ *Gary to Huntingburg* ➤• 45

FIVE •➤ *Indianapolis to Jeffersonville* ➤• 61

SIX •➤ *Kendallville to Logansport* ➤• 83

SEVEN •➤ *Madison to North Manchester* ➤• 93

EIGHT •➤ *Oakland City to Portland* ➤• 115

NINE •➤ *Ray to Syracuse* ➤• 121

TEN •➤ *Tampico to Vincennes* ➤• 137

ELEVEN •➤ *Wabash to Zionsville* ➤• 149

TWELVE •➤ *"Wish You Were Here"* ➤• 163

Bibliography   173

Index   175

Preface

Years ago I began saving old postcards. I was drawn to the history they preserved. As a primary means of communication for the common folk, they were a link to the past not found in history books or courthouse records. Many of the sites they depict have long since disappeared. Others have changed or deteriorated beyond recognition. A postcard may be the only surviving witness to the dirt road that used to be Main Street or the wooden bridge that once gave entrance to the park.

Despite the passage of so many years, the voices of these postcards still speak to us. The voices of the publishers are neatly presented in the captions, briefly detailing the images on the fronts of the cards. Much more intriguing are the voices of the people that have been preserved in the handwritten messages scrawled on the backs. Personal and poignant, immediate and evocative, they bring a snippet of the past to life, sharing with us times and places that we might otherwise never know.

Acknowledgments

My first and foremost appreciation to my life partner and wife, Claudette Swengel Reed, for her endless encouragement and tireless help with the details.

Special thanks also to Barry and Barbara Carter at the Knightstown Antique Mall and Nadine Abshire at the Glass Cupboard, both in Knightstown, Indiana, and to Jan Harvey at the National Road Antique Mall in Cambridge City, Indiana, for access to a great variety of wonderful old Indiana postcards. Additional thanks to Wayne Lawson and Phyllis Casey of Connersville, Indiana.

Last but not least a sincere thank you to Linda Oblack, assistant editor at Indiana University Press, for being so helpful, kind, and professional.

Introduction

Oh! The old swimmin' hole! When I
Last saw the place,
The scenes was all changed, like the
Change in my face.
—James Whitcomb Riley, "The Old Swimmin' Hole"

Much has changed in Indiana since the 1940s, when my grandfather used to drop my sister and me off in front of the old log jail in Nashville so that we could play while he attended to business and shopping chores. Back then, children could still play carefree on the courthouse lawn. The old log jail remains, but everything else in the town has changed.

The twentieth century has come and gone, but we can still catch glimpses of it in the old postcards that were sold in Indiana from the early 1900s onward. From Anderson and Angola to Wabash and Washington, Indiana postcards tended to showcase the points of interest or pride in the featured community. Depicting cities and towns, buildings and parks, postcards captured for future generations a landscape and way of life that would change irrevocably by the end of the century. In many cases the postcards themselves have barely survived, becoming tattered and worn through years of

The old log jail in Nashville. The town's second jail, it was built in 1879. Women were kept upstairs in the two-story building, and men were kept downstairs. Anyone entering the jail had to pass through three doors, the outer of which was padlocked and the innermost of which required the use of a ten-inch key. Ca. 1910.

handling and being tucked away in albums, boxes, and dresser drawers.

The postcard was well established in Europe before it came to the United States. The basic "Gruss aus" or "greetings from" postcard first appeared in the German States in the 1870s, following the onset of the Franco-Prussian War. A local view was featured on the front of the card, accompanied by the words "Gruss aus" followed by the location's name. By the late 1890s, the illustrated postcard had become popular in Great Britain as well. The Reverend Francis Kilvert wrote in his diary, "Today I sent my first postcards, to my Mother, Thersie, Emmie and Perch. They are capital things, simple, useful and handy. A happy invention."

In the early twentieth century, the "happy invention" arrived in the United States. Initially postcards were known here as "postals," after postal cards, which were issued in great numbers by the federal government during the last decade of the nineteenth century. Postal cards bore no pictures; the back was blank for a written message (or advertisement), and the front contained a space for the address and was stamped with the postage price. While there was a lot of room for the name and address of the recipient, plain postal cards did little to inspire either sender or receiver.

An act of Congress in 1898 authorized private printers to produce and sell picture postcards, with one restriction: the sender was not allowed to write anything other than the address on the back of the card. Personal messages were forbidden. Occasionally someone was bold enough to scrawl a brief note across the front just below or to the side of the image, but for the most part no personal comments accompanied the newly introduced view postcard.

In 1907, following the lead of several European countries, the United States Postmaster General acceded to the public's desire to include personal messages on the backs of postcards. The new cards used a vertical line to mark off the message space from the address space. Collectors call this a divided back postcard.

Once postcards could be used to convey news and announcements to recipients, and to share a sender's travels, they became a popular form of communication. Soon every store in every town in Indiana had a rack full of postcards for sale. In the larger communities, customers might be able to choose from a selection of striking images of important buildings and simple pastoral scenes. The smaller communities might offer nothing but stock postcards with the town name imprinted on them. But all were eagerly received by the folks back home.

As the number of available postcards increased, postcard collecting quickly became a national hobby. In the days before radio and TV, people entertained themselves by looking through their own and others' postcard albums. According to the U.S. postal authorities, almost 700 million postcards were mailed in the United States in fiscal year 1907–08—at a time when the entire population of the country was less than 89 million.

The postcard was a low-cost way to send a message—and to build a collection. The price of most of the better cards was just one cent; with another cent for postage, a card could be sent through the U.S. mail to just about anyone in America. At a time when few homes in Indiana had a telephone, the postcard was also a relatively rapid means of communication. By 1907, most rural areas had home mail delivery. No longer was it necessary for people to make a weekly trip to town to pick up their mail. With the help of the efficient national railroad system, it was not unusual for a postcard to be delivered elsewhere in the state the day after it was mailed—if the mail trains connected correctly. In some cases it might even be delivered the same day: a postcard mailed early in the morning at Jeffersonville might be delivered late the same evening in Terre Haute.

The quality of postcard images increased along with the popularity of this new form of communication. Some early picture postcards were printed in black and white. Collectors refer to these as "real photo" postcards. Others were color tinted, often with enhancements added to the image or distractions removed. Some of these stylized cards are true works of art. The better early postcards were printed in Germany, where the world's most advanced lithographic printing process was available. The quality of some of those cards was, and remains, remarkable. Crisp images were produced in striking color over the full surface of the front of the postcard.

After the onset of World War I in 1914, most American postcards were produced here at home instead of in Europe. In an effort to conserve on the use of costly inks, U.S. printers tended not to cover the entire printing surface on the face of a postcard, leaving a blank edge along each side. Collectors call these American-made postcards white border postcards.

During the 1930s, many of the postcards published in the United States were printed on paper with a very high rag content. The result was a surface with the look of quality linen. The image quality, however, was lower than in previous years. By the 1960s, the texture of these so-called linen postcards had given way to a smoothly finished glossy surface. These cards are known in collecting circles as chrome or chromes.

A postcard's type is not necessarily an accurate indicator of when it was mailed. Especially in a smaller store, a postcard might sit in the rack for years before being purchased and mailed. The postmark is the only reliable evidence of when it actually passed through the U.S. mail.

Professional printers needed an ongoing supply of interesting local views to produce the most appealing postcards. Most of the pictures were taken by professional photographers. While some came from local photographers, who maintained a studio in the featured community and made a living primarily by photographing distinguished citizens and their offspring, many were obtained from traveling photographers who moved from town to town, helping to provide the printing firms with the steady supply of images that they needed. A typical advertisement of the era called for photographers able to seek out "just what a tourist would readily buy as a souvenir of a visit. The view should be above all readily recognized as local—it should always include some familiar feature, building or landmark associated with the place." We have those photographers to thank for documenting thousands of views of Indiana in hundreds of locations. Without their efforts, many of those views would have been lost forever.

❧

The "golden age" of postcards, both in Indiana and in the United States in general, was the period from about 1907 to 1915. A number of factors contributed to their success. Of primary importance was the fact that postcards were big business and a source of profit for those who created and sold them, which ensured that there were a large number and a wide variety of interesting and high-quality cards for sale to meet the public demand. But a contributing factor was surely the greater mobility of the country's population. By this time interstate travel was becoming increasingly easier and more affordable. Nearly every town in Indiana had access to the railroad—and a train depot to prove it. By the early 1900s, the interurban, or electric railway, was connecting cities throughout the state with Indianapolis, making it relatively easy to journey to the "big city" and back in the same day. (Not surprisingly, train depots and interurban cars and tracks were a popular subject on Hoosier postcards of the time.) Travelers enjoyed being able to send friends and family postcards depicting the exotic and impressive sights in the areas they visited.

The postcard "craze" was winding down even before the onset of World War I. However, postcards remained a popular form of communication even after the war—and with more than 9 million automobiles registered in the United States by 1920, people were traveling even more. Postcards were cheap advertising for the thousands of motels, restaurants, and other businesses springing up along the highways from the 1920s through the 1940s, and stores and filling stations continued to stock good supplies of local views to sell to visitors.

By the 1950s, people were traveling fairly routinely. Communication was increasingly by telephone, and television and movies dominated the entertainment scene. Postcards were now relegated primarily to documenting people's vacation sites. Much had changed in Indiana, as in the rest of the nation, but thanks to the makers of postcards, we were left with a rich visual archive of days now gone. In forever recording the past of the Hoosier state, those vintage postcards continue to serve its history.

Patriotic greetings from Bono, a small community in Vermillion County near the western edge of Indiana. Ca. 1913.

"Greetings from Indianapolis" postcard. Postmarked 1942. Written message: "Dear Pal: You always send a very interesting card every time. Where do you get them? The weather has been colder this week which is better than all the heat we had. Hope to hear from you again soon. Yours truly, Evert."

*"Dear Pal: You always send a very interesting
card every time. Where do you get them? The
weather has been colder this week which is
better than all the heat we had.
Hope to hear from you again soon.
Yours truly, Evert."*

●❖

ong
may
he
ve!

Greetings from

Bono, Ind.

DIXIE ON L

Abraham Lincoln's Boyhood

RUSHVILLE
301
LINE

DRY GOO
C.F. ALLISO
READY

SOUTH SIDE INN

FEST & SON
FURNITURE

South

CABINS

ONE

Alexandria to Brazil

ALEXANDRIA

The Madison County town of Alexandria was laid out in 1836. By the next year a post office had been established there. After natural gas was discovered nearby in 1887, the town began to prosper, and it was chartered as a city in 1893. Although some of the factories left in the early 1900s, after the gas boom was over, a few thriving industries have remained.

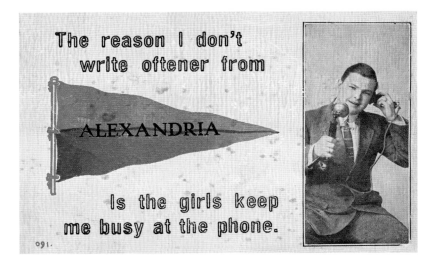

A greetings postcard from Alexandria. Even small communities could offer individualized stock cards such as this one. Early greetings postcards often featured a town's name superimposed on a pennant. Postmarked 1913.

ANDERSON

The seat of Madison County, Anderson is situated on the West Fork of the White River. Founded in 1823, it was known as Andersontown until 1844. Natural gas was discovered in the area in 1887, and by the 1940s the city had developed into a substantial industrial center. The Remy Electric Company built magnetos, generators, and other electrical items for the automotive industry. During World War II, the General Motors lamp plant made shell casings for the military. The city was also a busy railroad and interurban hub. In fact, it was an Anderson businessman, Charles L. Henry, who coined the word "interurban."

The prehistoric burial mounds at Mounds Park, located just outside Anderson, were a popular tourist attraction in 1909, when this card was mailed. Written message: "We are going to take our dinner to this park today."

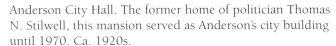

Anderson City Hall. The former home of politician Thomas N. Stilwell, this mansion served as Anderson's city building until 1970. Ca. 1920s.

Anderson High School. This landmark building burned in 1999. Ca. 1940s.

An aerial view of Anderson ca. the 1950s.

The *Gospel Trumpet* was the main journal for the Church of God, which has had its headquarters in Anderson since 1905. The Gospel Trumpet Company later became Warner Press. Ca. 1930s.

ANGOLA

Tucked away in the far northeastern corner of the state, just south of the Michigan border, Angola was incorporated as a village in 1838. The hilly terrain and numerous lakes in the area have long made the Steuben County seat a popular destination for vacationers, and in the first half of the twentieth century it was a nationally noted resort center. Pokagon State Park, which borders on Lake James and Snow Lake, is among the nearby attractions.

Two couples enjoy an outing on Lake James. Postmarked 1909. Written message: "Dear Cuz: How are you all? Have been so busy lately have not written you as I should have done. Hope you'll forgive me and write soon. Getting along nicely in school. Hope you're all well. Haven't heard from Reba for a long time. Spose she's mad? Love to all, Dawn."

The Lake Shore Depot in Angola was a busy place in summer as the trains unloaded passengers bound for the nearby lakes. Postmarked 1910. Written message: "Hello Blenn. Am at James. Will go home in a day or so. How about the mobile? Write to St. Joe."

Cars line up to visit a Sinclair gas station and the Hoosier Hills Observatory in Angola. Ca. 1930.

BEDFORD

The seat of Lawrence County, Bedford found itself in the national spotlight during the first half of the twentieth century as a major center for the limestone industry. Some of the most famous buildings in the nation have been constructed of Bedford limestone, including the Empire State Building, the Pentagon, and the National Cathedral. During the 1940s, visitors could take guided tours through the various stone quarries and mills. Decades later the city was still known as "the limestone capital of the world."

CUTTERS' DEPARTMENT, HOOSIER CUT STONE CO., BEDFORD, IND.

An interior view of the Hoosier Cut Stone Company in Bedford. Postmarked 1932.

D QUARRY, HOOSIER CUT STONE CO., BEDFORD, IND.

A quarry at the Hoosier Cut Stone Company, Bedford. Ca. 1920s.

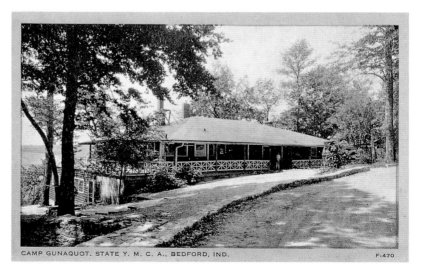

CAMP GUNAQUOT, STATE Y. M. C. A., BEDFORD, IND.   F-470

YMCA Camp Gunaquot, later renamed Camp Bedford. Ca. 1940.

BLOOMINGTON

The seat of Monroe County, Bloomington was settled in 1815. Only five years later, Indiana University was opened on the south side of town. Over the years, it would grow into a major educational institution. Although the university has always been the focal point in Bloomington, the city is also known for the nearby limestone quarries and Lake Monroe Reservoir, the largest manmade lake in the state. Native son Hoagy Carmichael composed his classic song "Stardust" in Bloomington. He is buried in the city's Rose Hill Cemetery.

Science Hall (now known as Lindley Hall) at Indiana University in Bloomington. Postmarked 1915. Written message: "Will you call on Mrs. Cocran (your new librarian) and her mother. They are to live with Miss Murphy. They are very nice women and you may be glad to have them. I told Mrs. Cocran that I would write."

The Monroe County Courthouse in Bloomington. The fish weathervane was made by Austin Seward, a Bloomington blacksmith. It had been placed atop the county's first courthouse in the late 1820s and was moved to this building after its completion in 1908. Ca. 1930s.

SCIENCE HALL, BLOOMINGTON, IND.

Monroe County Courthouse
Bloomington, Indiana

BLUFFTON

The seat of Wells County, Bluffton was named for its location on the bluffs overlooking the south bank of the Wabash River. Originally a small village, it began to grow in the late 1800s as a result of both the coming of the railroad and the discovery of oil in the area. By the early twentieth century, it was a highly regarded agricultural and dairying center. Charles Deam, the first state forester and a nationally recognized botanist, was born nearby.

Wells Co. Court House, Bluffton, Ind.

Jail, Bluffton, Ind.

The Wells County Courthouse in Bluffton. Completed in 1891, it is on the National Register of Historic Places. Postmarked 1909. Written message: "Dear Anna, Send your next letter to Muncie. As ever, Hattie."

(*left*) The old county jail in Bluffton. Jails and prisons were a popular subject on early postcards. Ca. 1910.

BRAZIL

Brazil was originally a stage line relay station, but it quickly benefited from its location along the new National Road (present-day U.S. 40), the first federally financed and constructed road in the United States, which was completed through Indiana in the 1830s. It became the Clay County seat in 1877 after the previous seat, Bowling Green, was deemed to be too far from the road. Brazil also benefited from its location in the heart of a clay- and shale-producing region, and by the middle of the twentieth century there were a number of large brick, sewer pipe, conduit, and tile plants close by. Nearby strip mines produced a variety of coal known as "Brazil coal."

Chicago Sewer Pipe Co., Brazil, Ind.

First M.E. Church, Brazil, Ind.

(*opposite top*) The Chicago Sewer Pipe Company was one of the first large clay-related industries to locate in Brazil, which was said to have an "almost inexhaustible supply of clay and shale." The company began operations there in 1893. Postmarked 1908. Written message: "Little Sweet, This will not interest you but it is quite a place and will help to fill your book. Papa."

(*opposite bottom*) The First United Methodist Church in Brazil was built in 1900. The towers have been remodeled some since this picture was taken. Postmarked 1908. Written message: "We arrived here at Indianapolis alright, tired but still ready for our train, which leaves at 3:35 a.m. We go by Columbus. Your children."

(*top right*) The business section of Brazil as it looked ca. 1913.

(*bottom right*) National Avenue in downtown Brazil as it looked ca. 1940.

"Little Sweet,
This will not interest you but it
is quite a place and will help
to fill your book.
Papa."

Business Section, Brazil, Indiana   13661   C. U. W. L. AMB. PARTLETT. BLOOMINGTON. ILL.

NATIONAL AVENUE, BRAZIL, INDIANA   H-448

Greetings from

Bono, Ind.

Abraham Lincoln's Boyhood

RUSHVILLE
301
LINE

C.F. ALLISO

SOUTH SIDE INN

South

CABINS

TWO

Greetings from INDIANA

Camp Atterbury to Dyer

CAMP ATTERBURY

Although it was not a town, the military center of Camp Atterbury had the population of a small city during World War II. Built in 1942 on more than 40,000 acres in Bartholomew, Johnson, and Brown counties, it housed and trained some 275,000 soldiers between then and 1946. It also served as an internment camp for thousands of Italian and German prisoners of war. The facility was inactivated in 1946, then reopened in 1950 for the Korean War. It closed again in 1955. Part of the camp continued to be used by the National Guard as a training facility. The Atterbury State Fish and Wildlife area occupies more than 6,000 acres that were eventually sold to the state.

GREETINGS FROM CAMP ATTERBURY, IND.

INTERIOR ARMY EXCHANGE, CAMP ATTERBURY, IND.

(*opposite top*) A greetings postcard from Camp Atterbury featuring a Douglas bomber with a "shark-like nose." Ca. 1940s.

(*opposite bottom*) Interior of the Army Exchange at Camp Atterbury. Ca. 1940s.

(*top right*) One of the barracks at Camp Atterbury. Ca. 1940s. Printed caption: "The most numerous of buildings are the neat rows of barracks, the soldiers' home away from home."

(*bottom right*) Fighting planes at Camp Atterbury. Ca. 1940s. Written message: "This might look that way from an airplane but it sure didn't look that way from the ground."

"*This might look that way from an airplane but it sure didn't look that way from the ground.*"

BARRACKS, CAMP ATTERBURY, IND.

GREETINGS FROM CAMP ATTERBURY, IND.

Division Headquarters at Camp Atterbury.
Ca. 1940s. Printed caption: "This is one of
the important military units stationed at
Camp Atterbury."

The Sports Arena at Camp Atterbury. Ca.
1940s. Printed caption: "The Sports Arena
is a spacious structure and supplies part of
the many recreational activities offered."

CANNELTON

The Perry County community of Cannelton was founded in 1837 by the American Cannel Coal Company. It was the county seat from 1859 until the early 1990s. Situated on the Ohio River, it was the site of the first Civil War action in Indiana when, in June 1863, a Confederate force crossed the river from Kentucky in an attempt to capture horses. Cannelton was home to the largest of the two cotton mills in Indiana, which operated from 1851 to 1954. Many of the town's buildings were destroyed in the Great Flood of 1937, which devastated communities along the Ohio. A flood wall was erected in 1950 for protection from future floods.

The Cannelton Cotton Mill was constructed of three-foot-wide blocks of native sandstone. Opened in 1851, it produced uniforms for the Union Army during the Civil War. It was designated a National Historic Landmark in 1991. In 2002 the building was converted into an apartment complex.

A view of Cannelton, with the Ohio River beyond. Ca. 1910.

Indiana Cotton Mills, Cannelton, Ind.

View of Cannelton, Ind.

COLUMBUS

Columbus was settled in 1820 and was selected as the seat of Bartholomew County the following year. It was originally known as Tiptonia, after General John Tipton, who had fought in the War of 1812. Located on the East Fork of the White River, it was a Union depot during the Civil War. Originally known for farming and milling, Columbus began to grow after the state's first railroad arrived in 1844. Known nationally for the production of Cummins diesel engines, automotive parts, and leather goods, the city also boasts buildings by a number of famous architects.

Bartholomew County Court House, Columbus, Ind.

9A382

Washington Street, South from Eleventh Street, Columbus, Ind.

(*opposite left*) Interurban tracks run down the center of Washington Street in Columbus. Postmarked 1908. Written message: "Hello Ernie: I am at Columbus Ind. Having a good time. Goodby. From Russ."

(*opposite right*) The Bartholomew County Courthouse in Columbus. Dedicated in 1874, it was built of foundation stone from quarries in North Vernon, finishing stone from quarries in Ellettsville, and brick from Indianapolis. Upon completion, it was declared by the *Louisville Courier-Journal* to be "the finest, most elegant and costly building in Indiana." Ca. 1912.

(*top right*) Central School, later Central Middle School, Columbus. Ca. 1920s.

(*bottom right*) The Irwin Home and Gardens have long been a favorite attraction in Columbus. The grounds were patterned after a garden in Pompeii, Italy. Joseph I. Irwin, who remodeled the house and added the gardens, was the founder of the Cummins Engine Company.

"Hello Ernie:
I am at Columbus Ind.
Having a good time.
Goodby. From Russ."

Central School, Columbus, Ind.

42759

The Irwin Home and Gardens, Columbus, Ind.

51190

The old City Hall building in Columbus. Completed in 1895 and for many years the hub of the city, it was later converted into an inn. Ca. 1920s.

The former public library in Columbus. It was replaced in 1969 by a new library designed by I. M. Pei. Ca. 1940s.

8. PARK SCENE AND CITY HALL, COLUMBUS, IND.

Public Library, Columbus, Indiana

73838

CONVERSE

The small Miami County town of Converse was originally known as Xenia. In 1892 it was renamed for the family of an early landowner. While traffic was often busy at the local Pan Handle (Pittsburgh, Cincinnati, Chicago and St. Louis Railway) railroad depot, which was a stop on the route from Columbus, Ohio, to Chicago, the overall population of the community was only around 900 in the early twentieth century. Several of the town's original brick buildings are on the National Register of Historic Places.

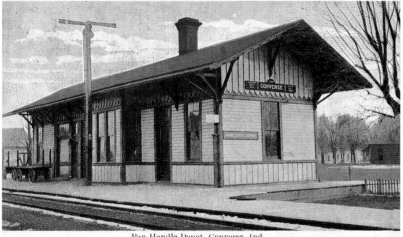

Pan Handle Depot, Converse, Ind.

The old Pan Handle railroad depot at Converse. This small frame depot was replaced in 1911 by a new brick depot, which was constructed nearby. Postmarked 1909. Written message: "Dear Louise: Will send you a card Dear and let you know if I feel alright I will be over Sunday. I will be there if possible if not I will be there next week Dear. I feel about the same and I hope I will hear from you today. Goodby Dear. Yours Forever Dear, John."

CORYDON

The small town of Corydon was the seat of the Indiana Territory from 1813 to 1816 and the first state capital from 1816 to 1825. It is now the seat of Harrison County. It was laid out on land purchased from William Henry Harrison, who also gave the town its name. Corydon was occupied by John Hunt Morgan and more than 2,000 of his Confederate Raiders in July 1863. The Battle of Corydon and the Battle of Gettysburg were the only two Civil War battles fought on Northern soil. The battle site and the state capitol building are on the National Register of Historic Places.

Old Constitutional Elm, in the shade of which Indiana's First Laws were Framed, Corydon, Ind.

The Old Constitutional Elm in downtown Corydon. The first constitution of the State of Indiana was written in its shade during the sweltering summer of 1816. Ca. 1910.

CRAWFORDSVILLE

The city of Crawfordsville was named for Colonel William H. Crawford, a famous Indian fighter from Virginia and a land agent for George Washington. The seat of Montgomery County, it is home to Wabash College. A popular attraction in Crawfordsville is the study of General Lew Wallace, a Civil War general and the author of *Ben-Hur*. Visitors to the Gen. Lew Wallace Study and Ben-Hur Museum can view the author's collection of books, paintings, and sculptures, as well as his Civil War uniforms. It is on the National Register of Historic Places, as is the city's old rotary jail, in which the cells rotate around a central steel cage to allow access to only one cell at a time. Closed in 1973, the jail is now a museum.

"Dear Judy, How are you making it by this time with LongBoy? Here is a picture of the place we are going to have a dance in on a week from next Sat eve. Write me a long letter. Bro Ernie."

Main Street, looking West, Crawfordsville, Ind.

A parade passes down Main Street in Crawfordsville. Ca. 1910.

The Gen. Lew Wallace Study and Ben-Hur Museum in Crawfordsville is a National Historic Landmark.

CULVER

Originally called Union Town, Culver was later renamed in honor of Henry Harrison Culver, the founder of Culver Military Academy. Throughout the twentieth century, the Marshall County town was home to only about 1,500 people, but with its location on Lake Maxinkuckee, the second-largest lake in Indiana, it has long been a popular tourist destination. More than 700 students attend the Culver Academies—the original Culver Military Academy and Culver Girls Academy, which was founded in 1971. The college preparatory schools are located on an 1,800-acre campus along the lake.

The Administration Building at Culver Military Academy. Postmarked 1950.

The Masonic Temple in Crawfordsville was built in 1902. Postmarked 1917. Written message: "Dear Judy, How are you making it by this time with LongBoy? Here is a picture of the place we are going to have a dance in on a week from next Sat eve. Write me a long letter. Bro Ernie."

THE COLOR GUARD, CULVER MILITARY ACADEMY, CULVER, IND.

3A-H721

Woodcraft Council Fire, Culver Summer Schools, Culver, Ind.

1B-H2337

THE CULVER BLACK HORSE TROOP, CULVER MILITARY ACADEMY,

CULVER, IND.

3A-H722

Culver cadets present the colors. Postmarked 1938. Written message: "Dear Charlotte— Saw the parade this noon, and it was quite a pretty sight. Will stop over at your place on the way back. Love, Katherine."

Culver has offered its Summer Schools program since the 1890s. The first Woodcraft Camp was held in 1912. The weekly council fire features American Indian stories, songs, and dances performed by the campers and instructors.

Culver's famed Black Horse Troop was formed in 1897. The troop has appeared in twelve presidential inaugural parades in Washington, D.C., beginning with the first inauguration of Woodrow Wilson in 1913, and has served as an escort to visiting royalty. Postmarked 1938. Written message: "Dear Grant, I'm surprised that you didn't drown. As a matter of fact, it was very brave of you to survive such a treacherous storm. Say—it won't be long before school starts and I dread the thought of going back. So long, Howie."

"Dear Charlotte—
Saw the parade this noon, and it was quite a pretty
sight. Will stop over at your place on the way back.
Love, Katherine."

A Review, Culver Military Academy, Culver, Ind.—27

The Culver cadets conduct a military review.

"Dear Grant,
I'm surprised that you didn't drown. As a
matter of fact, it was very brave of you to
survive such a treacherous storm. Say—it
won't be long before school starts and I dread
the thought of going back.
So long, Howie."

DYER

Founded in the 1850s, Dyer is situated in far northwestern Indiana, in Lake County near the Illinois state line. In the 1800s it was a busy railroad hub. Among the successful early businesses was the Hartman, Kallenberger and Gettler sauerkraut factory, whose products were sold throughout the Midwest. In the 1920s, the town drew national attention when an experimental highway was built from Dyer to Schererville. Only three miles long, it was called "the Ideal Section of the Lincoln Highway." The short stretch of road set the standard for later highway construction throughout the nation. Today Dyer is known primarily as a suburb of Chicago.

Greetings from DYER, IND.

43285

A greetings postcard from Dyer. Postmarked 1949.
Written message: "Hello. This town is first over state line so will send you one from Ind. instead of Ill. Monty."

DIXIE ON D

Abraham Lincoln's Boyhood

RUSHVILLE
301
LINE

DRY GOODS
C.F.ALLISO
READY

SOUTH SIDE INN

South

BEST & SON
FURNITURE

Greetings from

Bono, Ind.

my dear Nora:-
ibly come the
but well be a
Friday mor
Keep hard 9
gage our so
Eda & Mary,
will be there
be. Many &
coming pure
W-C-1
Ede & Mary are
coming (P.) We w
we were too

CABINS

VORIS & FISHER PRINT

THREE

Elkhart to French Lick

ELKHART

Elkhart, in Elkhart County, was founded in the 1830s and incorporated as a city in 1875. Situated at the confluence of the Elkhart and St. Joseph rivers, near the Michigan border, it was a major railroad junction by the middle of the nineteenth century, and it quickly grew into one of the largest industrial cities in the state. Elkhart has long been known as "the band instrument capital of the world"; at one time there were eleven instrument factories in the city. In the twentieth century it also earned the nickname "RV capital of the world" for the hundreds of manufacturers in the area who produce recreational vehicles and parts.

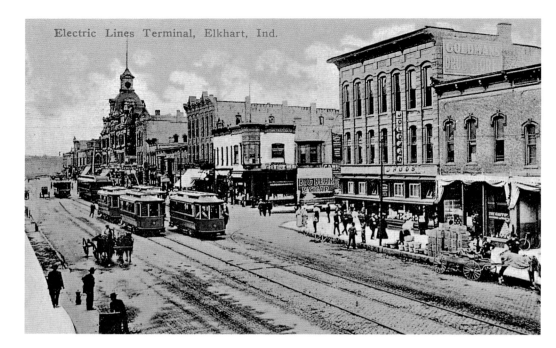

Electric Lines Terminal, Elkhart, Ind.

MCNAUGHTON PARK BRIDGE, ELKHART, IND.—35

(*opposite top*) Interurban cars share the street with horses and pedestrians in early Elkhart.

(*opposite bottom*) The McNaughton Park Bridge in Elkhart. Printed caption: "One of the most beautiful concrete structures crossing St. Joseph River, was erected at a cost of $131,000.00. It is an important link in Elkhart's traffic system."

(*top right*) Rice Field, now used by Elkhart Central High School. Printed caption: "This stadium, with a seating capacity of 8,500, is part of 94 acres donated to the city by the late James Addison Rice. The field is located along the Elkhart River and is among the finest school athletic fields in the state."

(*bottom right*) Elkhart's Main Street was a busy place in the early 1950s.

RICE ATHLETIC FIELD OF ELKHART HIGH SCHOOL, SHOWING ELKHART RIVER, ELKHART, IND.—32

Main Street, Elkhart, Indiana

ELWOOD

Founded in 1853, the Madison County town of Elwood was originally known as Quincy, and then as Duck Creek. It was renamed for the final time in 1869. Initially a small town, Elwood benefited from the natural gas boom of 1887. As manufacturers moved into the area over the following years, it grew into a thriving trade and industrial center. On the national scene, Elwood is best known as the birthplace of politician Wendell Willkie. A corporate executive with no previous political experience, Willkie won the Republican nomination for president in 1940, then went on to lose decisively to President Franklin Roosevelt. At the time, his 22 million votes were the largest number ever earned by a Republican presidential candidate.

WENDELL WILLKIE   H-425

MRS. EDITH WILLKIE   H-426

BOYHOOD HOME OF WENDELL WILLKIE, ELWOOD, INDIANA

ELWOOD PUBLIC LIBRARY

WHERE MRS. WILLKIE WAS LIBRARIAN BEFORE MARRIAGE   H-428

(*opposite left*) Elwood native Wendell Willkie. Ca. 1940s.

(*opposite right*) Edith Willkie, the wife of Wendell Willkie.

(*above*) Wendell Willkie's boyhood home.

(*right*) The Elwood Public Library, where Edith Willkie worked. A Carnegie Library, it was dedicated in 1904. It was replaced in 1997 by a new building across the street.

ENTRANCE TO HIGH SCHOOL BUILDING

THE HOPE OF OUR COUNTRY

WHERE WENDELL WILLKIE GRADUATED, ELWOOD, INDIANA   H-427

MANGAS CAFETERIA, ELWOOD, INDIANA

(*left*) The high school in Elwood from which Wendell Willkie graduated. The building burned in 1988, and this arch was later incorporated into the town's new high school/middle school complex.

(*above*) Mangas Cafeteria, Elwood. Ca. late 1940s. Printed caption: "Best place to eat in the Middle-West. Steaks and chops, Air-conditioned. Corner of Main and Anderson Streets Elwood, Indiana."

EVANSVILLE

The seat of Vanderburgh County, in the far southwestern part of the state, Evansville was settled in the early 1800s. A busy Ohio River port and railroad hub, it is also known as an industrial center and the heart of a prosperous coal-mining and agricultural region. It is home to two universities—the University of Evansville (founded in 1854) and the University of Southern Indiana (founded in 1965). Two-time Indiana governor Robert Orr was born in Evansville.

Evansville began to develop into a major port city after the last stretch of the Wabash and Erie Canal was completed in 1853, linking the Ohio River at Evansville with Lake Erie at Toledo, Ohio. The canal failed not too many years thereafter, but Evansville continued to thrive. Ca. 1910.

The Southern Indiana Hospital for the Insane later became Evansville State Hospital. Asylums were a poplar subject on early postcards. Ca. 1913.

Boat Landing, River Front, Evansville, Ind.

Southern Indiana Hospital for the Insane, Evansville, Indiana.

Trinity (Catholic) Church and School, Evansville, Ind.

Greyhound Bus Station.

(*left*) The Holy Trinity Catholic Church in Evansville. Ca. 1913.

(*above*) The Greyhound bus station was one link in Evansville's busy transportation system in the 1940s.

(*right*) Evansville's Main Street was busy even at night in 1940, at which time the city had a population of more than 110,000.

(*below*) Bosse High School was one of some thirty schools in Evansville in the 1940s.

Night Scene, Main Street, Evansville, Indiana

Air View, Bosse High School and Enlow Field, Evansville, Indiana

FAIRMOUNT

The Grant County community of Fairmount was originally called Pucker. Settled primarily by Quakers, it was laid out in 1850. The town is nationally known as the home town of actor James Dean; he was born in nearby Marion, but his parents moved to Fairmount shortly after his birth in 1931. Almost fifty years after his death in a car accident at the age of 24, fans still visit his gravesite in Park Cemetery. A James Dean Festival is held every fall.

Henley Ave., Fairmount, Ind.

Henley Avenue, Fairmount. Postmarked 1909. Written message: "Dear Cecil. Well how are you? You must be dead. I have been so busy I couldn't come out. Mable had a baby girl and I am helping her. The baby died. Come out when you can. With <u>lots</u> of love, Margaret."

FORT BENJAMIN HARRISON

Fort Benjamin Harrison, in Marion County, was named for the twenty-third president of the United States, who served from 1889 to 1893. Harrison was not a native Hoosier, but he lived in the state for much of his life and was a distinguished resident of Indianapolis. The fort was established as a military post in 1903 and played a major role in the training of soldiers during World Wars I and II. In the 1940s it was one of the largest army posts in the country.

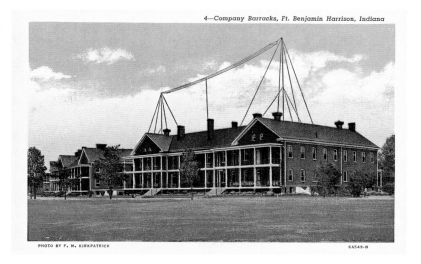

4—Company Barracks, Ft. Benjamin Harrison, Indiana

PHOTO BY F. M. KIRKPATRICK   6A549-N

Company barracks at Fort Benjamin Harrison. Postmarked 1942. Written message: "Dear Dad, I am going on kitchen duty. I have to make my own beds. I feel OK. Miss you and mom. Don't write because I am leaving in a day or two. Hope you are OK. Love, Hugh."

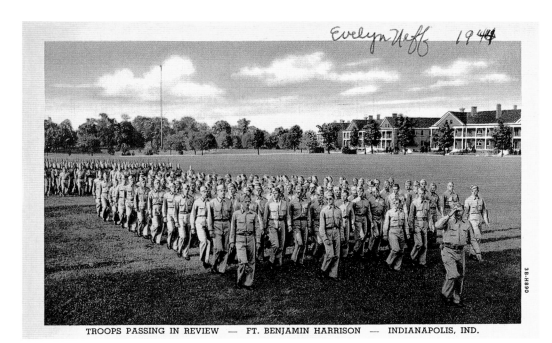

Evelyn Neff 1944

TROOPS PASSING IN REVIEW — FT. BENJAMIN HARRISON — INDIANAPOLIS, IND.

2—Officers' Quarters, Ft. Benjamin Harrison, Indiana

PHOTO BY F. M. KIRKPATRICK   6A547-N

Troops passing in review at Fort Benjamin Harrison. Postmarked 1944. Written message: "Hello, hello, Greetings from the Army. Been in 2 weeks and still like it. You ought to see me drill—wow!! Don't know where I'll go next, but I'm ready. Love, Evelyn."

The officers' quarters at Fort Benjamin Harrison. Ca. 1940s.

"Hello, hello, Greetings from the Army. Been in 2 weeks and still like it. You ought to see me drill—wow!! Don't know where I'll go next, but I'm ready. Love, Evelyn."

❦

FORT WAYNE

The seat of Allen County, Fort Wayne was established on the former site of a Miami Indian village. It was platted in 1824 and named for General Anthony Wayne, who had built a stockade on the site in 1794. Situated where the St. Joseph and St. Mary's rivers come together to form the Maumee, the city began to thrive after the arrival of the railroads and canals. By the 1940s it was a major industrial center and transportation hub. Numerous celebrities were born in Fort Wayne, including actresses Carole Lombard and Shelley Long, designer Bill Blass, and Philo T. Farnsworth, who invented television. It is also the birthplace of baking powder, the gasoline pump, and the hand-held calculator. Johnny Appleseed is buried in David Archer's Cemetery, two miles north.

Home for the Feeble-Minded, Fort Wayne, Ind.

NO. 3 FIRE STATION, FT. WAYNE, IND.

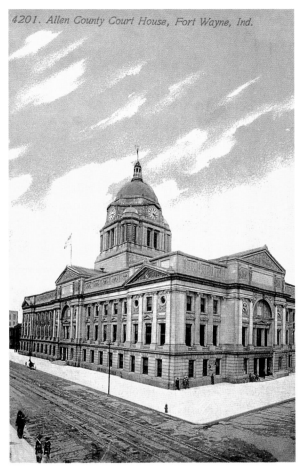

4201. Allen County Court House, Fort Wayne, Ind.

10948. St. Mary's Bridge, Fort Wayne, Ind.

*"Dear Bro and All, We got home all OK at 11 o'clock. Had one puncture about 15 miles from Ft. Wayne, got along just fine. Hope Cora feels better.
Ans. to Toledo 1543 Erie St.
Freda and Geo."*

(*opposite top*) The State Home for the Feeble-Minded was moved to this building in Fort Wayne in 1890. It later became the Fort Wayne Developmental Center. Postmarked 1909. Written message: "Received your P.C. All OK and hoping you will like this one in return."

(*opposite bottom*) Engine House No. 3 served Fort Wayne's business district. It was retired in 1972 and now houses the city's Firefighters' Museum. Postmarked 1914.

(*left*) The Allen County Courthouse in Fort Wayne. Dedicated in 1902, it cost $817,553.59 to build. It was renovated in the late 1990s at a cost of $8.6 million. Postmarked 1913. Written message: "Having a great time over here, Sun set in the east and come up in the west. Gladys."

(*above*) An interurban car sits on a bridge over the St. Mary's River in Fort Wayne. Ca. 1910.

41. CALHOUN STREET, LOOKING NORTH, FORT WAYNE, IND.

(*above*) Calhoun Street, Fort Wayne. Postmarked 1922. Written message: "Hello Kid: How are you, I am well, hoping you the same. I suppose you are going to school by this time. I have quit school. I have nothing to do at present time but write letters and cards to my friends. Went to the store last night, was good too. OK Kid."

(*right*) Waiting for a train to arrive at the Pennsylvania Railroad Depot in Fort Wayne. Postmarked 1916. Written message: "Dear Mother, Why don't you write me. I have sent you a card and a letter since I came to Ft Wayne. Have got a fine job, like it fine, calling in the Pennsylvania Train House making 2$^{\underline{00}}$ per day. 457 Wallace St. Bye Bye."

Waiting Room. Pennsylvania Depot. Fort Wayne, Ind.

LINCOLN TOWER, BY NIGHT, FORT WAYNE, IND.

IA-H296

The art deco Lincoln Bank Tower in Fort Wayne was the first skyscraper built in Indiana. Completed in 1930, it was the tallest building in the state until 1969. Postmarked 1937.

BIRD'S-EYE VIEW OF GENERAL ELECTRIC CO. PLANT, EAST OF BROADWAY, FORT WAYNE, IND.   51319-C

A General Electric plant in Fort Wayne. GE has had a major presence in the city since the late 1800s. Postmarked 1931.

"Hello Kid: How are you, I am well, hoping you the same. I suppose you are going to school by this time. I have quit school. I have nothing to do at present time but write letters and cards to my friends. Went to the store last night, was good too. OK Kid."

FRANKFORT

Frankfort was laid out in 1830. In the early 1900s it was a typical picturesque Indiana town. By mid-century the Clinton County seat had grown into a busy trade and food-processing center. It is the birthplace of actor Will Geer.

Frankfort's Main Street offered a typical view of Middle America in 1907, when this card was mailed. Most people still traveled by horse and buggy, but the automobile would soon make its way to town. Written message: "Received yours yesterday. We are not coming this eve. Will leave for Kansas on 15 and will write when get back. Having a good time. Don't write to Indiana."

MAIN STREET LOOKING NORTH, FRANKFORT, IND.

FRANKLIN

The city of Franklin was founded in 1823 and named for Benjamin Franklin. The seat of Johnson County, it began to thrive after the arrival of the Madison and Indianapolis Railway in 1846 and developed into a trade and shipping center. In the 1940s it was the center of a booming tomato-canning industry. It is the birthplace of two Indiana governors, Paul McNutt and Roger Branigin. Franklin College was founded in 1834 under the direction of the Indiana Baptist Education Society. In 1842 it became the first college in the state to admit women.

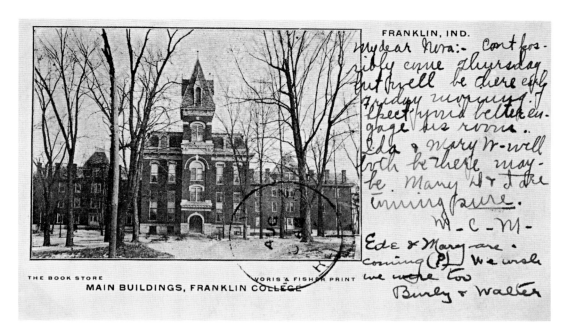

THE BOOK STORE

MAIN BUILDINGS, FRANKLIN COLLEGE

Franklin College. Postmarked 1905. Written message: "My dear Nora: Can't possibly come Thursday but will be there early Friday morning. I expect you'd better engage us rooms. Ida and Mary W. will be there <u>maybe</u>. Mary D. and I are coming <u>sure</u>. M. C. M. Ede and Mary are coming (P). We wish we were too. Burly and Walter."

The former Franklin High School. This section of the building was torn down in the 1980s. Postmarked 1912.

Fountain erected by Raper Commandery No. 1, K. T., Indiana Masonic Home, Franklin, Ind.

JEFFERSON STREET, FRANKLIN, INDIANA   N-352

(*top left*) The Indiana Masonic Home in Franklin has served as a retirement community for Indiana Masons and their families since 1916. Postmarked 1924.

(*bottom left*) Jefferson Street in Franklin as it looked ca. 1940.

(*opposite top*) A garden at the French Lick Springs Hotel. Postmarked 1946. Printed caption: "French Lick Springs, in the Cumberland Hills of Southern Indiana, is the home of the world famous Pluto Water, and is America's famous health and pleasure resort." Written message: "Dear Boy, Do you like this waterfall and pond? I had a grand train ride out here. I had a bed on the train. Take care of Mother and the girls. Love, Daddy."

(*opposite bottom*) An aerial view of the French Lick Springs Hotel. Postmarked 1954. Printed caption: "French Lick is but a few miles from the center of population of the United States."

FRENCH LICK

Recognized by many today as the home town of legendary basketball player Larry Bird, the Orange County town of French Lick was a nationally known resort town in the nineteenth and early twentieth centuries, famous for its acclaimed Pluto, Bowles, and Proserpine mineral springs. Water from its Pluto Spring was bottled and sold throughout the United States and in many other parts of the world. The French Lick Springs Hotel (later renamed the French Lick Springs Resort and Spa) housed thousands of visitors annually in its 470 rooms, including Al Capone and Franklin D. Roosevelt. It was also a training site for boxing champion Joe Louis. It celebrated its 100th anniversary in 2002. Visitors to the spa today can still enjoy a bath in the hot Pluto Mineral Springs.

"Dear Boy, Do you like this waterfall and pond? I had a grand train ride out here. I had a bed on the train. Take care of Mother and the girls. Love, Daddy."

"The Home of Pluto Water"

Lily Pond in Garden, French Lick Springs Hotel, French Lick, Ind.   124154-N

"The Home of Pluto Water"

French Lick Springs Hotel, French Lick, Ind.   124156-N

ony
may
she
ve!

Greetings from

Bono, Ind.

DIXIE ON

Abraham Lincoln's Boyhood

RUSHVILLE
301
LINE

C.F. ALLISO

SOUTH SIDE INN

South

CABINS

VORIS & FISHER PRINT

FOUR

Greetings from **INDIANA**

Gary to Huntingburg

GARY

The Lake County city of Gary, in the far northwestern corner of the state, was founded in 1909 on 9,000 acres along Lake Michigan that had been purchased the previous year by the U.S. Steel Corporation. It was named for the chairman of that company's board of directors. The land was chosen for its proximity to Chicago, its easy access to lake and rail transportation, and its good water supply. The port city grew rapidly and prospered in the heyday of the U.S. steel industry; within a decade of its founding, its population had reached 25,000. After the decline of the steel industry in the late twentieth century, Gary had to begin to re-create itself. In recent years it has become a popular destination for tourists wanting to visit the city's casinos and the nearby beaches along the Indiana Dunes National Lakeshore.

Broadway Street in Gary, with an interurban car and tracks at center.

Inside the engine room at the Indiana Steel Company (the Gary Works plant of the United States Steel Corporation). Postmarked 1913.

Fifth and Broadway, Gary, Ind.

LOOKING EAST ON FIFTH AVE.,
SHOWING KNIGHTS OF COLUMBUS CLUB HOTEL,
GARY, IND.—56

A view of Gary from the corner of Fifth and Broadway. Ca. 1920.

The Knights of Columbus Club Hotel in Gary. Built in 1925, it was later renovated as an apartment building. It is on the National Register of Historic Places. Ca. 1930. Printed caption: "The imposing ten-story Knights of Columbus Club Hotel, the first set-back type of architecture in the city, was erected in 1926 at a cost of $2,000,000. It is one of the finest club hotels in the state with 120 rooms for men. In addition to its magnificent lodge rooms, it includes a swimming pool, bowling alleys, ballroom and smaller recreational parlors."

VIEW OF STEEL MILLS, GARY, INDIANA

Jackson Street South from Sixth Ave., Gary, Ind.

(*top left*) A split view of the steel mills in Gary. Ca. 1930s.

(*above*) Blast furnaces at the U.S. Steel Corporation in Gary. Ca. 1940s.

Less than fifty years after its founding, according to author Henry Alsberg, Gary had grown "from a group of tar-papered shacks to a metropolis with planned residential districts and a school system of national note." Ca. 1940s.

GENEVA

Novelist Gene Stratton-Porter may not have put Geneva on the map, but her success as a writer made the Adams County town a tourist attraction. Nearby, at the headwaters of the Wabash River, was the swampy area known as Limberlost country, which she wrote about in works such as her well-known novel *A Girl of the Limberlost*. Stratton-Porter lived in Geneva for more than twenty-six years, until the swamp was drained. Her fourteen-room home there is now a State Historic Site, the Limberlost State Memorial Cabin.

Gene Stratton-Porter's cabin in Geneva.

GENTRYVILLE

The tiny Spencer County town of Gentryville was platted in 1854. It was named for James Gentry, a merchant originally from North Carolina who settled in the area in 1818. Abraham Lincoln spent his youth in Spencer County, from ages 7 to 21, and as a teenager he worked as a clerk in Gentry's store. In 1844, Lincoln delivered a campaign speech in Gentryville, at the home of his lifelong friend Colonel William Jones. That house is now a designated State Historic Site. The Lincoln Boyhood Home National Memorial and Lincoln State Park are in nearby Lincoln City.

Abraham Lincoln's boyhood home near Gentryville, now the Lincoln Boyhood Home National Memorial. Lincoln's mother is buried there. Ca. 1910.

GOSHEN

Goshen, the seat of Elkhart County, was platted in 1831. Located within a rich agricultural area along the Elkhart River, it is home to large Amish and Mennonite communities, and also to a growing Hispanic community. Goshen College is one of the few Mennonite-sponsored colleges in the country. The Mennonite Historical Library is located on its campus.

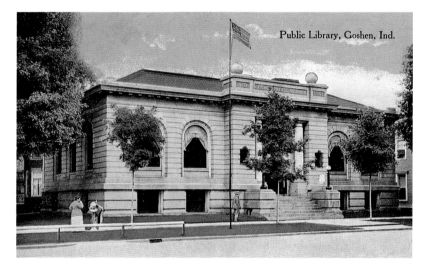

The former Goshen Public Library. Dedicated in 1903, it was one of the Carnegie Libraries, financed by philanthropist Andrew Carnegie. A new library was built in 1968, and the mayor's office was moved into this building. Postmarked 1916. Written message: "Dear Helen, Arrived O.K. Fishing and boating fine. Was so cold here last Sun. we had to build a fire in our heating stove. My regards to all. Write. Yours, O."

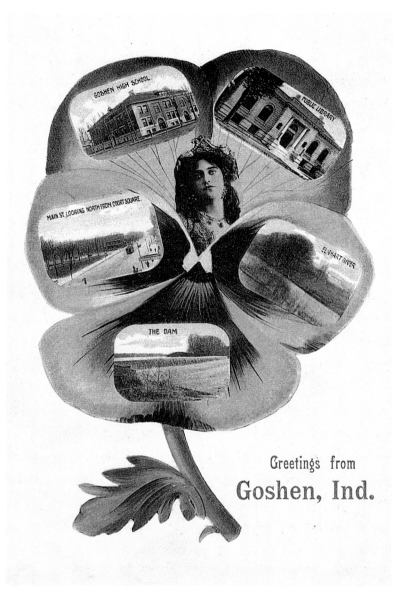

An early greetings card from Goshen. The pansy's petals showcase Goshen High School, the Public Library, the Elkhart River, "the dam," and Main Street. Written message: "Dear Geraldine. News rec'd. Good luck to both you and Babe. Hope to see you soon. Aunt Allie."

Jefferson Theatre, Goshen, Ind.

6806. M. E. Church, Goshen, Ind.

Generations of Goshenites attended stage shows, vaudeville shows, and movies at the Jefferson Theatre (later the Goshen Theatre) on Main Street. Postmarked 1923. Written message: "Hitting the road hard and fast, am well but lonely. Not much further to go today but have to make haste, for little time to complete this job. Kind of thinking of paying another flying visit to you. Cheerio. Hope all well, Regards, Sed."

The First United Methodist Church in Goshen has changed very little since this picture was taken. It was built in 1874. Ca. 1918.

Goshen's Main Street ca. the 1940s.

"Hitting the road hard and fast, am well but lonely. Not much further to go today but have to make haste, for little time to complete this job. Kind of thinking of paying another flying visit to you. Cheerio."

Main Street, Goshen, Ind.

GREENFIELD

Greenfield was a tiny town when it was chosen as the seat of Hancock County in 1828. A decade later, it began to benefit from its location on the National Road (present-day U.S. 40), and by 1876 it had grown enough to be incorporated. It was a thriving city for twenty years after the gas boom of the late 1800s, during which time it became home to a number of industries. Today it is best known as the birthplace of the beloved "Hoosier poet," James Whitcomb Riley. The old Riley home was restored and became an early tourist attraction. It is on the National Register of Historic Places.

The boyhood home of James Whitcomb Riley, Greenfield. Ca. 1918. Written message: "Dear Mrs. Boone, Dad and Eck. How are you all? We got here all O.K. But we are all in with the load we had. James don't like the country any better than before. Bert is working and I don't know when we will be home. With love to all. Good By. Jeanie."

James Whitcomb Riley's Home. Greenfield, Ind. 2417

Court House, Greenfield, Ind.

GREENSBURG

The Decatur County seat of Greensburg was settled in 1822. Over the years, it developed into a trade center for the surrounding agricultural area. It was also known for the quality of its limestone quarries. The nearby Harris City Stone Quarry produced the "blue limestone" that was used in the construction of the Indiana State House in Indianapolis, the U.S. Customs Building in Cincinnati, Ohio, and the Proctor & Gamble soap factory near Cincinnati. Greensburg is perhaps best known for the series of trees that have grown out of the roof of the Decatur County Courthouse since the early 1870s. How the first tree took root there and how they are nourished is not known, but they continue to draw curious tourists to the town.

(*above*) The Hancock County Courthouse in Greenfield. Constructed of Indiana limestone, it was completed in 1898. A statue of James Whitcomb Riley was erected out front in 1918. Ca. 1916.

(*right*) Main Street in Greensburg. Postmarked 1906.

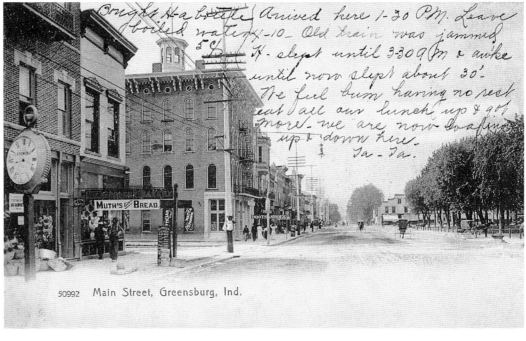

50992 Main Street, Greensburg, Ind.

The IOOF Home in Greensburg. It was later torn down and replaced by a retirement home. Postmarked 1914.

The former Greensburg High School. The site where it stood became a parking lot when a new school was built nearby. Ca. 1915.

B462B7   I. O. O. F. Home, Greensburg, Ind.

154   HIGH SCHOOL, GREENSBURGH, IND.

LONE TREE ON COURT HOUSE TOWER, GREENS-BURG, IND. is unparalleled in the world. The present tree is about 13 years old, but one or more trees have been growing on this tower for over 50 years.

Court House Tower, Greensburg, Ind.

85478-N

COURT HOUSE TOWER SHOWING TREE GROWING OUT OF ROOF.

GREENSBURG, IND.

E-543

Two views of a tree growing out of the roof of the courthouse tower in Greensburg. Ca. 1920s.

HAMMOND

Hammond was the first town established in the Calumet Region. Platted in 1875 and incorporated in 1884, the Lake County city was named for George H. Hammond, whose successful slaughterhouse was the first industry to locate in the area. He also pioneered the shipment of beef by refrigerated rail car. When he died in 1886, his wife sold the slaughterhouse to an English syndicate for $6 million. With its ideal location on Lake Michigan and its extensive connections as a transportation hub, Hammond prospered as both a thriving resort town and a busy industrial center. Other successful businesses over the years have included the Pullman-Standard plant, which produced railroad cars from 1929 to 1981, and the Lever Brothers Company, which has done its part to clean the world with products such as Lux, Pear, Rinso, Lifebuoy, and Dove soap.

A bird's-eye view of Hammond. Postmarked 1914.

Along Lake Michigan in Hammond. Written message: "Dear Bro, Just a line. Am back on the job. Haven't examined the spot yet down the river, may go tomorrow—have you caught any since I left. With love, Ellsworth."

Looking Northwest from Court House Clock Tower, Hammond, Ind.

Summer Days, Lake Michigan, Hammond, Ind.

HANOVER

A charming small town in Jefferson County, Hanover lies along the scenic Ohio River, in a rich agricultural region. It is best known as the home of Hanover College, the oldest private college in the state. Located on a high bluff overlooking the river, the coeducational Presbyterian-affiliated school was founded in 1827. In earlier times, the number of students often surpassed the population of the town.

HARTFORD CITY

The seat of Blackford County, Hartford City was founded in 1839 and incorporated in 1857. It was an agricultural center until the 1890s, when the Indiana gas boom transformed it into a business and industrial center. At one time there were eleven glass manufacturers in the city, most of which are now gone.

OHIO RIVER FROM COLLEGE CAMPUS, HANOVER, IND.

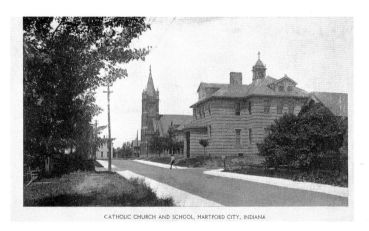

CATHOLIC CHURCH AND SCHOOL, HARTFORD CITY, INDIANA

The Ohio River at Hanover. Postmarked 1936. Written message: "Dear Marjorie: This is the scene which we saw during vespers last night. It is really nice. Am having fine time and meeting many new and interesting people. There are 24 from Rush Co. More than twice as many as from any other co. Will tell you about it when I get home. Jane."

(*top right*) St. John the Evangelist Catholic Church and School in Hartford City. The school building was torn down and replaced in the mid-1950s. Postmarked 1907. Written message: "Dear Iva, Am very sorry we can't be there Sunday 13 as I have been visiting of late and will have to stay at home for a few weeks to make-up what I have lost. Yours Respt., Walter."

The Odd Fellows Building and Masonic Temple in Hartford City. Ca. 1910.

HIGHLAND

Located in Lake County in extreme northwestern Indiana, Highland was a tiny community along an old Potawatomi trail until the establishment of a railroad station there in 1882. Originally called Clough, it was renamed in 1888. It was incorporated in 1910. Highland grew rapidly during the first half of the twentieth century. Its population quadrupled between 1930 and 1950—from 1,500 to 6,000—and fifty years later it had quadrupled again..

Bob's Tourist Court, a motel in Highland. Ca. 1950. Printed caption: "Indiana's Finest Motor Court. Open year around. 35 modern units—12 heated garages, 9 kitchenettes. Hardwood floors and Venetian blinds. Centrally heated, 27 miles South of Chicago's Loop. Family accommodations—Your comfort guaranteed."

Congles Restaurant Lounge, Highland. Ca. 1950s. Printed caption: "U. S. Routes 41 and 6—Highland, Indiana. Steaks, chicken and fish dinner parties and weddings. Jim Congles, Mgr.—Tel. Highland 825."

BOB'S TOURIST COURT

9117 WICKER PARK BLVD. — HIGHLAND, IND.

8B-H1358

U. S. ROUTES 41 and 6
HIGHLAND, INDIANA

HUNTINGBURG

Founded in 1839, the small town of Huntingburg in Dubois County was so named because it was the favorite hunting ground of Colonel Jacob Geiger, one of the area's first permanent settlers. Huntingburg is nationally noted for the production of Uhl pottery. The Uhl family settled in the area in 1908, drawn by the area's pure clay deposits. The company shipped stoneware throughout North America until the 1940s. Parts of the Tom Hanks film *A League of Their Own* were filmed at Huntingburg's old baseball park, Huntingburg League Stadium.

Huntingburg Memorial Gymnasium was originally part of Huntingburg High School. After that school was torn down, the gymnasium continued to be used by Southridge High School. Ca. 1950s. Printed caption: "Evansville Central vs. Huntingburg—Attendance 7,000. This beautiful gym is an example of Indiana's interest in basketball. The seating capacity is about twice the population of the city. Dedicated Nov. 13, 1951; it was necessary to add seats in 1954."

FIVE

Indianapolis to Jeffersonville

INDIANAPOLIS

The state capital and the seat of Marion County, Indianapolis was settled in 1820 on a site one mile square that was chosen for its central location. The downtown was laid out around a circular plaza, which was originally called Governor's Circle, and a mansion was built there for the governor. It was such a public location, however, that no governor wanted to live in the home, and it was razed in 1857. The towering Soldiers and Sailors Monument was erected on the plaza in 1902, and the circle was given the name Monument Circle. It is still the heart of the "Circle City" today.

Despite the lack of a navigable waterway, Indianapolis quickly grew into a transportation and manufacturing center. The completion of the National Road (present-day U.S. 40; Washington Street in Indianapolis) through the state in the 1830s, followed a decade later by the coming of the railroads, brought a steady stream of settlers and industries to the capital. In the early 1900s, the city was also a busy interurban hub, with electric railway lines radiating out in all directions.

With the growing popularity of the automobile in the early twentieth century, Indianapolis soon became a center for the automotive industry. Over the years, more than seventy different cars were produced in the city, including the Stutz, the Duesenberg, the Cole, the Empire, the Premier, the Waverly, and the Marmon. The nearby Indianapolis Motor Speedway was built in 1909 as a testing track for cars and equipment. In 1911 it became the site of the first running of one of the most famous sporting events in the world, the Indianapolis 500. That year's race was won by Ray Harroun, who was driving a Marmon "Wasp."

Today Indianapolis still thrives as a commercial and transportation hub and a business and financial center. It has grown from the original square mile to a total land area of more than 3,500 square miles. Kurt Vonnegut, David Letterman, Jane Pauley, and jazz great Wes Montgomery were born in Indianapolis, and among those buried in its Crown Hill Cemetery are Benjamin Harrison, James Whitcomb Riley, Booth Tarkington, Colonel Eli Lilly, and John Dillinger.

Crown Hill, east entrance, Indianapolis, Ind

8063. HOTEL ENGLISH AND ARMY AND NAVY MONUMENT, INDIANAPOLIS, IND. COPYRIGHT, 1904, BY DETROIT PHOTOGRAPHIC CO.

(*opposite*) Crown Hill Cemetery was dedicated on June 1, 1864. The East Entrance opened in October of that year.

(*above*) The Soldiers and Sailors Monument and the English Hotel, on Monument Circle in Indianapolis. Postmarked 1905. Written message: "Will come tomorrow if it is a pretty day on the car (interurban), leaving Indianapolis at 9:30 a.m."

(*right*) The Indiana Pythian Building in Indianapolis was completed in 1906, the year this card was postmarked. It was torn down in the 1960s and replaced by the Indiana National Bank Building.

INDIANA PYTHIAN BLDG., INDIANAPOLIS.

INDIANAPOLIS, State Soldiers and Sailors Monument.   777·

8/23-07. Am here hustling Scottie.

(*left*) The 284-foot-tall Soldiers and Sailors Monument was a favorite subject on early postcards. Postmarked 1907. Written message: "Am here hustling, Scottie."

CHRIST CHURCH AND THE COLUMBIA CLUB.   BOARD OF TRADE AND HUME MANSUR BUILDINGS

Christ Church, the Columbia Club (*far right*), the Board of Trade Building (*behind Christ Church*), and the Hume Mansur Building (*behind the Columbia Club*) in downtown Indianapolis. Completed in 1859, Christ Church is the oldest building on Monument Circle. The Columbia Club was founded in 1889 by supporters of Benjamin Harrison, the twenty-third president of the United States. They originally called themselves the Benjamin Harrison Marching Society. This building was replaced by a larger one in 1925, which was designed by Rubush and Hunter, who were also the architects for the Murat Temple, the Circle Theatre, and the Hume Mansur Building. Postmarked 1920.

"Am here hustling, Scottie."

The former Marion County Courthouse in Indianapolis was completed in 1887. It was replaced by a twenty-eight-story office building in 1962. The City Market and Tomlinson Hall, shown to the left, were built in 1886. The marketplace was still going strong at the end of the twentieth century, but Tomlinson Hall was demolished after a fire in the 1950s. Postmarked 1907. Written message: "Dear Mrs. H.— Would like if you would answer my return mail and tell me if you are home. Have you seen Babe yet. Sister is still here, going home Sun. Henry McG is very sick. We have a telephone. The 'old' same as the Bell in C. C. Our number is Prospect 1255 if you should ever want us. Ella."

The former headquarters of the Indianapolis Fire Department, located at the corner of Massachusetts and New York streets. Ca. 1910.

"Dear Mrs. H.— Would like if you would answer my return mail and tell me if you are home. Have you seen Babe yet. Sister is still here, going home Sun. Henry McG is very sick. We have a telephone. The 'old' same as the Bell in C. C. Our number is Prospect 1255 if you should ever want us. Ella."

MARION COUNTY COURT HOUSE (TOMLINSON HALL & CITY MARKET AT LEFT), INDIANAPOLIS, IND.

Fire Department Headquarters, Indianapolis, Ind.

The entrance to Woodruff Place in Indianapolis. Laid out in 1872–73, the planned residential subdivision was designed to look like a park. Its mansions were home to such luminaries as author Booth Tarkington and artist T. C. Steele. It deteriorated badly after the Depression but has since undergone a process of preservation and restoration. Postmarked 1908.

The old Claypool Hotel in Indianapolis. It closed after a fire in 1967 and was demolished two years later. Postmarked 1908.

Woodruff Place Entrance, Indianapolis, Ind.

Claypool Hotel, Indianapolis, Ind.

Traction Terminal, Indianapolis, Ind.

The Indianapolis Traction Terminal. Opened in 1904, it grew to be the largest interurban terminal in the world. Some 7 million passengers passed through its gates every year. It later was used as a bus terminal. The huge shed was demolished in 1968, and the building was torn down four years later. Postmarked 1908. Written message: "Dear Sis! Well Ada this room is as I expected. The woman and not the room is what took his eye. Clean they don't know what clean means here. If my girl is good and you want her till Xmas OK. We may be back up here by then. Alice."

An interurban car speeds down the track. Interurbans were the mass transit of their day.

An "Indiana Limited" (70 miles an hour), Indianapolis, Ind.

"Dear Sis! Well Ada this room is as I expected. The <u>woman</u> and not the room is what took his eye. <u>Clean</u> they don't know what clean means here. If my girl is good and you want her till Xmas OK. We may be back up here by then. Alice."

❧

(*above*) Riverside Boulevard in Indianapolis. Postmarked 1909.

(*right*) The former Canoe Club at Riverside Park in Indianapolis. Postmarked 1909.

In the early 1900s, Washington Street in Indianapolis was shared by trolley cars, horse-drawn carriages, bicyclists, and pedestrians. Postmarked 1909.

A night-time view of Washington Street. Postmarked 1910. Written message: "Dear brother. I am having a fine time. Seen the Wright Brothers fly their air ships this afternoon. How is everybody. Will see you in 30 days. Pearl."

"Dear brother.
I am having a fine time.
Seen the Wright Brothers fly
their air ships this afternoon.
How is everybody.
Will see you in 30 days.
Pearl."

Washington Street looking East from Meridian Street, Indianapolis, Ind.

WASHINGTON STREET (AT NIGHT) INDIANAPOLIS, IND.

(*right*) Indianapolis, looking northeast from Monument Circle. Postmarked 1910.

(*below*) The Murat Temple and Theatre opened in downtown Indianapolis in 1910, the year this card was postmarked. It was restored to its original splendor in the 1990s. Written message: "Dear Grandma: We arrived here all right. It is a lovely cool day. We are waiting for the train to Springfield. Love to all. Abbie."

Bird's Eye View, Northeast from Monument Place, Indianapolis, Ind.

Murat Temple and Theatre, Indianapolis, Ind.

"Dear Grandma: We arrived here all right. It is a lovely cool day. We are waiting for the train to Springfield. Love to all. Abbie."

RACING STABLES, STATE FAIR GROUNDS, INDIANAPOLIS, IND.   11150

So you go next year?

P.R.S.

(*left*) Racing stables at the Indiana State Fairgrounds in Indianapolis. Postmarked 1912. Written message: "Things in the <u>fair</u> line start going tomorrow. I will try to take in some of it but don't think I will enjoy fair folks here as in Shelbyville. P. R. S."

(*below*) The IOOF Building was located at the corner of Washington and Pennsylvania streets in downtown Indianapolis. Ca. 1910.

"Things in the <u>fair</u> line start going tomorrow. I will try to take in some of it but don't think I will enjoy fair folks here as in Shelbyville. P. R. S."

❧

I. O. O. F. Building,   Indianapolis, Ind.

G 27013 Pleasure Boat "Sunshine", Broad Ripple Park, Indianapolis, Ind.

Broad Ripple Park, Indianapolis. Post-marked 1914.

An early view of the business district in downtown Indianapolis.

Real Estate Row, Market Street East from Pennsylvania St., Indianapolis, Ind.

James Whitcomb Riley's Residence, Indianapolis, Ind.

The Indianapolis home of James Whitcomb Riley. Ca. 1920. Printed caption: "Where the famous poet lived and completed many of his works, including 'Lockerbie Street,' a tribute to the little street on which the home is located. The home has been preserved as it was when the poet resided there and is open to visitors."

The State House in Indianapolis. Completed in 1888, it cost $2 million to build. Ca. 1930s.

12:—Indiana State Capitol, Indianapolis, Ind.

The Riley Hospital at Indianapolis, Ind. — D-16

SEVERIN HOTEL, INDIANAPOLIS, IND.

3A-H762

(*above*) Riley Hospital, Indianapolis. Ca. 1940s. Printed caption: "Erected in memory of James Whitcomb Riley, the beloved 'Hoosier Poet.' This institution specializes in the treatment of physically handicapped children and is equipped with an occupational therapy workshop and a hydrotherapeutic pool. The art glass windows and wall decorations portray Riley's poems."

(*right*) The Severin Hotel opened in downtown Indianapolis in 1913. The historic thirteen-story building was renovated in 1995. Postmarked 1941.

The Field House, Butler University, Indianapolis, Indiana   14

(*above*) Butler Fieldhouse (later renamed Hinkle Fieldhouse) at Butler University in Indianapolis. When the facility opened in 1928, it was the largest basketball arena in the nation. The home of the Indiana Boys' High School Basketball Tournament from 1928 to 1971, it was the site of the most famous basketball game in Indiana history—the historic final game in 1954, in which a last-second shot by Hoosier legend Bobby Plump gave tiny Milan High School a one-point victory over powerhouse Muncie Central. It is a National Historic Landmark. Ca. 1940s.

(*right*) The Hotel Warren, Indianapolis. In 1983 it was renamed the Canterbury Hotel. Ca. 1940s. Printed caption: "Indianapolis' newest hotel, fireproof, 250 rooms with tub or shower, all outside, excellent food, outstanding tap room, entertainment, parking lot, garage. Rates from $2.25."

HOTEL WARREN, Indianapolis, Ind.

CADLE TABERNACLE, INDIANAPOLIS, IND.

41946

Indianapolis Motor Speedway.
The Greatest Race Course in the World.

Cadle Tabernacle, Indianapolis. Opened in 1921 as the headquarters of evangelist E. Howard Cadle, it seated 10,000 and had room in the choir loft for 1,500. In addition to hosting such famous evangelists as Billy Sunday, Aimee Semple McPherson, and Billy Graham, it served as an important site for cultural and educational events in the city. It was demolished in 1968. Postmarked 1947. Written message: "Dear Mommie and Dick, Got my load off and am loading 700 feet at Gulfport Mississippi. And I am suppose to load in Kansas City for Erie so I should be home Monday or Tuesday. Hope I can find something for Dick's birthday. Love, Dad."

The Indianapolis Motor Speedway. Postmarked 1909. Printed caption: "The Speedway Park is an area of 328 acres. Total cost over $350,000. Circumference of outer track and road course, five miles. Grand stands and boxes will accommodate 25,000. Entire grounds will accommodate 200,000. Ten thousand automobiles can be parked on the grounds."

The Indianapolis Motor Speedway ca. 1940.

The Indianapolis Motor Speedway ca. the 1950s. Printed caption: "Indianapolis Motor Speedway, the site of the annual 500 mile Automobile speed Classic, is located on West Sixteenth Street (State Road 34). Built in 1909, and improved yearly, the Track is a two and one-half mile paved oval. The World's greatest Race Course draws some 150,000 people on the yearly Memorial Day Race."

JEFFERSONVILLE

The seat of Clark County, Jeffersonville was founded in 1802 on the site of an earlier settlement at Fort Steuben. Its layout was based on a grid plan created by Thomas Jefferson, and the city was named in his honor by William Henry Harrison. The city benefited from its location on the Ohio River, attracting a number of industries, including the maker of Louisville Slugger baseball bats. It was a center for the steamboat industry in the nineteenth century. The Howard Ship Yards were a major boat-building firm in the 1850s; 150 years later, as Jeffboat, Inc., the company was the largest inland shipbuilder in the nation.

"Dear Mom,
Maurice feels a little better. Are you
going to the country Sunday or will
you be home, let me know and we
will be up either Sun or Mon. We
had a good rain here but still is hot.
Write so I'll get it Sat.
Love, Dot and Maurice."

Indiana Reformatory, JEFFERSONVILLE, Ind.

(*opposite*) The Indiana Reformatory in Jeffersonville was built in 1847. It later became a soap factory. Postmarked 1909.

(*top right*) The former Clark County Courthouse in Jeffersonville. It was replaced in 1960 by the City-County Building. Ca. 1910.

(*bottom right*) The Big Four Bridge between Louisville and Jeffersonville. Built in the 1890s, it was the site of two construction accidents that claimed sixty-one lives. Postmarked 1936. Written message: "Dear Mom, Maurice feels a little better. Are you going to the country Sunday or will you be home, let me know and we will be up either Sun or Mon. We had a good rain here but still is hot. Write so I'll get it Sat. Love, Dot and Maurice."

Clark County Court House, Jeffersonville, Ind.   A-14909-N

BIG FOUR R. R. BRIDGE BETWEEN LOUISVILLE, KY. AND JEFFERSONVILLE, IND.   V 277   76697

EAST CHESTNUT STREET, CORNER, LOCUST BY NIGHT.

SPRING STREET AND COURT AVENUE.

Street Scenes in Jeffersonville, Ind.

Two views of early Jeffersonville.

The Great Flood of 1937 was one of the worst floods in U.S. history. It devastated towns throughout the Ohio River Valley. "Disaster postcards" such as these were popular, capturing important historical images for future generations. (*right*) The post office, the library, and the Citizens Trust Company in Jeffersonville during the flood. (*bottom right*) The U.S. Quartermaster Depot in Jeffersonville. When it wasn't underwater, it supplied equipment to the U.S. military. (*below*) Main and Fourth streets in Jeffersonville after the flood.

525   Post Office, Library, Citizens Trust Co., Jeffersonville   Jan. 1937

302   Main and Fourth, Jeffersonville, Ind.

529   U. S. Q. M. Depot, Jeffersonville, thought to be above flood stage Jan. 1937

ony may she ve !!

Greetings from

Bono, Ind.

DIXIE ON

Abraham Lincoln's Boyhood

RUSHVILLE 301 LINE

C.F. ALLIS

SOUTH SIDE INN

South

CABINS

My dear Neva:—

FRANKLIN COLLEGE

VORIS & FISHER PRINT

SIX

Kendallville to Logansport

KENDALLVILLE

The Noble County town of Kendallville was settled around 1832. It was named for General Amos Kendall, who served as U.S. Postmaster General under President Andrew Jackson. In the early twentieth century, it was known for its factories and its fishing. It was also a regional center for the surrounding agricultural area.

"Dear Oka, I will send you a postal, which leaves me well and having lots of sleigh rides. Hope you are too. Write Soon, Your Friend Blanch."

The Flint and Walling Manufacturing Company in Kendallville. One of the oldest pump companies in the nation (est. 1866), it was at one time a major manufacturer of windmills. Postmarked 1910. Written message: "Dear Oka, I will send you a postal, which leaves me well and having lots of sleigh rides. Hope you are too. Write Soon, Your Friend Blanch."

Works of Flint & Walling Mfg. Co., KENDALLVILLE, IND.

KNIGHTSTOWN

Knightstown was laid out in 1827 and incorporated in 1837. The small Henry County community was named for Jonathan Knight, the chief surveyor for the National Road, which ran nearby. Knightstown lies in an agricultural region that produces livestock and grain. Located midway between Indianapolis and Richmond, it attracted a number of industries and businesses in its early years, and by the early twentieth century it was a railroad and interurban hub. It is the birthplace of historian and educator Charles Beard.

Bird's Eye View of S. and S. O. Home, Knightstown, Indiana.   3523   BANKER'S STUDIO.

The Soldiers' and Sailors' Orphans' Home in Knightstown was founded in 1865 to care for orphaned and destitute children of Civil War veterans. Ca. 1912.

The office of the *Knightstown Banner* and a printing office. The *Banner* was founded in 1867. Postmarked 1941.

KOKOMO

Founded in the mid-1840s, the Howard County seat of Kokomo was named for a Thorntown Miami Indian chief. After natural gas was discovered in the area in 1886, the city enjoyed rapid industrial growth. It was the home of Elwood Haynes, who is credited with building one of the earliest American automobiles, in 1894. By 1916, Haynes was producing 7,000 cars a year. The first pneumatic rubber tire was invented in Kokomo in 1894, by the president of the Kokomo Rubber Tire Company. By the 1950s, the city was well known for the manufacture of metal and glass products. Grissom Air Force Base is nearby.

An auto rally in Kokomo. The Frances Hotel, now gone, was one of the largest hotels in the city. Ca. 1910.

The City Park bandstand in Kokomo. Postmarked 1911. Written message: "Dear Aunt, Don't think hard of me for not writing sooner. Am busy washing and canning fruit, I don't have time to even eat. I do five family washings a week and all extra care. I got ten Post Cards is every body well we are well. Lou."

Frances Hotel, Kokomo, Ind.

BAND STAND IN CITY PARK, KOKOMO, IND.

KRAMER

The Warren County town of Kramer was originally called Cameron. Its name was changed to Mineral Springs in 1889, and then to Kramer in 1901, after Henry Kramer, who had built a posh resort hotel in the town called Mudlavia. The springs on the site were said to have "curative properties" related to the treatment of "all diseases of the kidneys, blood, skin and nerves." Tourists and celebrities flocked to the resort to take the waters. The hotel burned in the 1920s and was never rebuilt. In the 1990s, water from the springs began to be bottled and sold.

The hotel at Mudlavia. Visitors to the resort were given souvenir postcards to mail to their friends.

The spring house at the Mudlavia health resort in Kramer, near Attica. Ca. 1915. Written message: "Here is one of the spring houses out of a dozen or more. Any time you go there there are hundreds of people there bring there dinner and spend the day. It is an enjoyable place to be especialy such hot days as yesterday and to day. I can't hardly stand it I am so warm."

MUDLAVIA HOTEL, ATTICA, INDIANA   F-406

Spring House, Mudlavia, near Attica, Ind.

LAFAYETTE

Lafayette was named in honor of France's Marquis de Lafayette, who was touring the United States at the time of the city's founding in 1825. The following year it was chosen as the seat of Tippecanoe County. In 1859, it was the site of the first official airmail flight attempted by the U.S. Postal Service. Professor John Wise went aloft in a balloon, carrying a mail pouch containing 123 letters and 23 circulars. Bound for New York, he ran into problems with the wind and made it only to Crawfordsville, where he handed off the mail to a passing train. Lafayette is located in a rich agricultural region that was noted by the 1950s for its dairies and grains. Purdue University, in the adjoining city of West Lafayette, was founded in 1869.

The Lafayette Post Office in the early 1900s. It was torn down and replaced in the 1930s.

The Wabash Valley Sanitarium, Lafayette. The grounds later became the site of Wabash Valley Hospital in West Lafayette. Postmarked 1908. Written message: "Dear Hazel: I will write to you now. I would of written when I wrote the other girls but I knew you were in the country and I thought I would wait till this week. G.W."

"On the Banks of the Wabash"

WABASH VALLEY SANITARIUM
On the Lawn   La Fayette, Ind.

COURT HOUSE, LA FAYETTE, IND.—7

The Tippecanoe County Courthouse in Lafayette. Completed in 1884, it was the largest construction project in Indiana at the time. The dome is topped by a statue of Liberty. Postmarked 1948. Written message: "Dear Friend— Thanks for nice card. Sis went home Sun. Sure miss her. We took a short trip Sat. Enjoyed it so much. L.F. is one of the places. It has so many interesting places to see. Purdue University is one. Also old soldiers home. Lovely parks and stores. Best wishes, B.T."

The Memorial Union Building at Purdue University. Postmarked 1953. Printed caption: "One of the most complete and finest student buildings in the U. S. is the Memorial Union Building at Purdue University. It provides ample facilities for all extra curricular organizations and activities on the campus and also has a hotel wing with 126 rooms."

Memorial Union Building,
Purdue University, Lafayette, Ind.

"Dear Hazel:
I will write to you now. I would of written when I wrote the other girls but I knew you were in the country and I thought I would wait till this week.
G.W."

LA PORTE

The city of La Porte was founded by French pioneers in 1830. Two years later it was chosen as the seat of La Porte County. It was incorporated as a town in 1835. With a number of lakes and parks nearby, La Porte has long been a popular resort area. A young journalist named Ernie Pyle worked as a cub reporter for the *La Porte Herald* before moving to Washington, D.C., and embarking on the career that would turn him into the nation's most famous war correspondent during World War II.

LOGANSPORT

The Cass County seat of Logansport is situated at the junction of the Wabash and Eel rivers. Located in a productive agricultural area, it is home to a number of manufacturers. Two makes of cars, the Bendix and the Revere, were manufactured there in the early twentieth century. A number of the town's buildings are on the National Register of Historic Places, as is the Spencer Park Dentzel Carousel, now located in Riverside Park. The carousel's forty-two hand-carved animals, some of which are more than a hundred years old, were carefully restored. The annual Iron Horse Festival celebrates the town's history as a railroad hub.

Court House, La Porte, Indiana

1727—Post Office, Logansport, Ind.

(*opposite left*) The La Porte County Court-house in La Porte. Completed in 1894, it was built of Lake Superior red sandstone, which was shipped by boat to Michigan City, and from there by rail to La Porte. Postmarked 1944.

(*opposite right*) The old Logansport Post Office. Built in 1905, it was used until the 1960s. In 2003 the building was being used as a law office and had been partially restored to its original condition. It is part of the Courthouse Historic District, which was added to the National Register of Historic Places in 1999. Postmarked 1906.

(*top right*) The former Cass County Court-house in Logansport. In 1979 it was replaced by the four-story Cass County Building. Postmarked 1910.

(*bottom right*) An early view of Spencer Park in Logansport. Postmarked 1911.

Court House, Logansport, Ind.

SPENCER PARK, LOGANSPORT, IND.

5946.

Greetings from

Bono, Ind.

DIXIE ON L...

Abraham Lincoln's Boyhood

RUSHVILLE 301 LINE

C.F. ALLIS...

SOUTH SIDE INN

FURNITURE

South

CABINS

SEVEN

Greetings from
INDIANA

Madison to North Manchester

MADISON

Madison, the seat of Jefferson County, was settled around 1805, making the Ohio River port city one of the oldest communities in the state. It was the first city in Indiana to have a municipal water system. Early travel guides directed visitors to the town's large tobacco warehouses around Central and West streets. Tourists were also drawn to Madison's numerous historic homes, several of which are on the National Register of Historic Places. Clifty Falls State Park opened nearby in 1920.

The City of Madison, Madison, Ind.

Clifty Inn, Clifty Falls State Park, Madison, Ind.

A bird's-eye view of early Madison.

Clifty Inn at Clifty Falls State Park, Madison. Postmarked 1930.

MARENGO

The small Crawford County town of Marengo is located on the Big Blue River, near the Hoosier National Forest. The town had one of the first interurbans (in 1893), but it is known primarily for Marengo Cave, one of the most spectacular show caves in the Midwest and a National Landmark. It was discovered in 1883 by a group of children playing in a sinkhole. With its huge main corridor, its abundance of stalactites and stalagmites, and its underground rivers containing blind fish and crayfish, Marengo Cave has long drawn both admiration and tourists.

Greetings From Marengo. Ind.

A greetings postcard from Marengo. Postmarked 1916.

MARION

The city of Marion was settled in 1826 on the banks of the Mississinewa River. In 1831 it was chosen as the seat of Grant County. It was named for the "Swamp Fox," Francis Marion, a cavalry officer in the Revolutionary War. After the discovery of oil and gas in the area in the late 1800s, the city's economy boomed. Its population boomed accordingly: Between 1880 and 1900, the number of residents increased more than fivefold, from around 3,000 to more than 17,000. Over the years Marion attracted a number of industries, including Crosley Motors, the manufacturer of the nation's first compact car. Seven miles north is the Mississinewa Battlefield, the site of the first U.S. victory in the War of 1812.

The Grant County Courthouse in Marion. The dome and the statue of Lady Justice on top were removed in 1943, after a fire. Postmarked 1909. Written message: "Did you say winter, well I should guess. I have just taken a position at a grocery store and am not in the city very much. If you want to leave any word at the Gallery for me you may. I am still Ernest."

Matter's Park, Marion, Ind.

The "Flowing Well" in Marion's Matter Park was a popular attraction in the early 1900s. Postmarked 1907.

By 1909, when this card was postmarked, an increasing number of visitors to the park were coming by car.

"Did you say winter, well I should guess. I have just taken a position at a grocery store and am not in the city very much. If you want to leave any word at the Gallery for me you may. I am still Ernest."

The entrance to the former National Soldiers' Home in Marion. The home was established by an act of 1890 to care for disabled Civil War veterans. With the addition of a number of new buildings, the site was still being used as a VA hospital more than a hundred years later. Ca. 1910.

The old YMCA building in Marion. It was torn down and replaced by a parking lot. Postmarked 1913.

Marion, Indiana. Entrance to National Soldiers Home.

Marion, Indiana. Y.M.C.A. Building.

MARSHALL

The Parke County town of Marshall was platted in 1878. It was named for Mahlon Marshall, who had donated land there for a railroad station. Marshall is best known as the home of Turkey Run State Park, which was established in 1916 as Indiana's second state park. Its deep sandstone gorges and old growth forests have made it a popular tourist destination and hiking spot ever since. A narrow suspension bridge crosses Sugar Creek, and there are a number of historic buildings in the park, including an old gristmill that is on the National Register of Historic Places. Marshall also has its share of historic covered bridges.

(*top*) The Idyl Wyld Roller Palace in Marion opened in 1937. It was still a popular spot in the early twenty-first century. Ca. 1940.

(*bottom*) Martin Boots Junior High School in Marion. Martin Boots and David Branson donated the land for Marion in 1831. The school was later demolished, and an apartment complex was built on the site. Ca. 1940s. Printed caption: "Marion has an excellent school system, well equipped modern buildings, also owns the Memorial Coliseum with an athletic field house."

The Turkey Run Inn opened in 1919 at Turkey Run State Park in Marshall. At one time, excursion trains regularly brought guests in from Chicago. Ca. 1940s. Printed caption: "Owned by the State and managed by Jack C. Lenhart, the inn has 128 bedrooms and dining room facilities for 450 people. Home of Hoosier Food and Hoosier Hospitality."

MARTINSVILLE

The Morgan County seat of Martinsville was laid out in 1822. It was still a small town during the early twentieth century, but it had a big reputation nationally because of its artesian mineral springs and accompanying sanitariums. At one time there were twelve sanitariums in operation in the town. People flocked to the area in great numbers to take the waters, which were believed to have healing properties. The last spa, Home Lawn Mineral Springs, closed in 1971.

The New Highland Mineral Springs Sanitarium, Martinsville, Ind.

4A-H714

First Presbyterian Church in Martinsville. Ca. 1910.

(*left*) The Highland Sanitarium in Martinsville. Completed in 1929, the five-story brick building had terrazzo floors, a Mexican adobe lobby, Spanish-style light fixtures, and large arches in the corridors. It was later converted into an apartment complex. Ca. 1930s.

PRESBYTERIAN CHURCH, MARTINSVILLE, IND.

MICHIGAN CITY

Situated on the south shore of Lake Michigan, in La Porte County, Michigan City was incorporated in 1836. The port city had a population of 1,500 at the time, with a thriving commercial district, and it would soon see even more growth with the coming of the railroads. The Haskell-Barker Car Company, later Pullman-Standard, made railroad cars in the city for many years. Another thriving industry was the Indiana State Prison, where many of the inmates were under contract for labor. With its location in the popular Dunes area, its superior transportation connections, and extensive recreational facilities that included parks, theaters, and pageants, Michigan City also developed into a popular resort area.

"Dear saster,
We are all well and hope you are
the same. I am going to have
a quilting and wont you
to come the 22th of February.
Try and get all to getter and come.
I have rote to all."

Greetings from Michigan City, Ind.

Dress Suit Case Series   Copyrighted 1908 by Franz Huld Co. N. Y.

A greetings postcard from Michigan City. Dated 1908.

Entrance to Indiana Prison, Michigan City, Indiana.

The Indiana State Prison at Michigan City. Ca. 1910. Early postcards identified it as the Northern Indiana State Prison, "a model penal institution."

Spring Street, Michigan City. Ca. 1912.

PUBLISHED BY GEO. LEUSCH, MICHIGAN CITY, IND.   11599
SPRING STREET SOUTH FROM SEVENTH STREET,
MICHIGAN CITY, IND.

Excursion Boat at Dock, Michigan City, Ind.

Excursion boats from Chicago brought thousands of passengers to Michigan City each weekend during the early twentieth century. Postmarked 1918. Written message: "Have been quarreling with Harvey all day. He wants me to erase it but I won't. With love, Vivian."

Sheridan Beach at Michigan City began filling up with summer homes during the first few decades of the twentieth century.

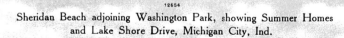

12654
Sheridan Beach adjoining Washington Park, showing Summer Homes and Lake Shore Drive, Michigan City, Ind.

"Have been quarreling with Harvey all day. He wants me to erase it but I won't. With love, Vivian."

Fishing for perch at Michigan City. The lighthouse at the end of the pier was completed in 1904. Postmarked 1924.

Monkey Island at the Washington Park Zoo in Michigan City. Established in 1928, it is one of the oldest zoos in Indiana. Printed caption: "Washington Park, Michigan City, Ind., On Lake Michigan. The beauty spot of Northern Indiana with its Sand Dunes, Flower Gardens, Playgrounds and Zoo. The Monkey Island located at the Hillside in the Zoo. Pictured on the other side of this card is the feature attraction."

WHEN THE PERCH ARE BITING AT MICHIGAN CITY, IND.

The Monkey Island, Washington Park, Michigan City, Ind.

COPYRIGHT BY GEO. LEUSCH

Showing the Beautiful Hillside Flower Gardens and Waterfalls

2B-H514

MIDDLETOWN

The Henry County community of Middletown was laid out in 1829. It was named for its location midway between Anderson and New Castle. A small crossroads town during the first half of the twentieth century, it had its own grain elevator and very little traffic.

MITCHELL

The settlement that became the small Lawrence County town of Mitchell dates to approximately 1813. Originally known as The Crossing, and later as Woodland, it was re-named Mitchel (the second "l" was added later) in 1854, in honor of Major General Ormsby McKnight Mitchel, the chief engineer for the Ohio and Mississippi Railroad. The town was incorporated in 1864, and the city in 1907. It is the birthplace of Gus Grissom, one of America's first astronauts, who died aboard the *Apollo 1* capsule in 1967. Nearby Spring Mill State Park features a restored pioneer village with a working gristmill.

Locust Street, Middletown, Ind.

Locus Street, Middletown. Postmarked 1909.

(*right*) Flower Garden and Hamer's Mill at Spring Mill State Park, Mitchell. Postmarked 1946. Written message: "Dear Mamma: I am alone in living r. writing. John gone to bed, Henry to a LAV meeting, and Bob to town to library or ?. I have a dental date in am. Rose helped iron today. I'll sign this off and retire. Just happened to have this card at home here. Hope you are OK and have someone by now. As ever, Edna, Henry, Bob and John B."

Flower Garden and Hamer's Mill,
Spring Mill State Park, Mitchell, Indiana

MOORESVILLE

The Morgan County town of Mooresville was laid out in 1824 by Samuel Moore, a drygoods merchant who had opened a store nearby. A Quaker, he would not allow the lots to be publicly sold; instead he gave them to people he considered desirable. Mooresville was home to two famous people: an early baseball player, pitcher Amos Rusie (1871–1942), a native son of Mooresville who was known as the "Hoosier Thunderbolt"; and John Dillinger, the infamous bank robber, who spent his teenage years on a nearby farm. A small community for much of the twentieth century, Mooresville had grown to a population of close to 10,000 in 2000 as a result of its proximity to Indianapolis.

West Main Street, Mooresville. Postmarked 1909. Written message: "Dear Sister and Brother, Was glad to hear from you and was more than glad to receive the little Xmas present you sent me. It was just what I have been wanting. It is so nice to use with my Sewing Machine. Come and see me when you can. Good Bye from Cora."

Indiana Street, Mooresville. Postmarked 1910.

VIEW ON WEST MAIN STREET, MOORESVILLE, IND.

View on S. Indiana Street, Mooresville, Ind.

MORGANTOWN

The Morgan County community of Morgantown was settled in 1831 near the site of a mill. It was a sleepy Hoosier village until State Road 135 opened in 1935, which linked Morgantown with Nashville and Brown County State Park. Travelers have long stopped to marvel at the Rock House, which was built in 1894 by James "Smith" Knight. Built of cement blocks embedded with rocks, coins, marbles, jewelry, dishes, and toys (including a ceramic doll head), the landmark building was later converted into a bed and breakfast.

MOUNT VERNON

The Posey County seat of Mount Vernon was settled around 1800 and platted in 1816. Originally known as McFadden's Bluff and McFadden's Landing, after the town's first settler, it was later renamed for George Washington's home in Virginia. Mount Vernon is located on the Ohio River in the far southwestern corner of the state. A number of its buildings and archaeological sites are on the National Register of Historic Places.

GREETINGS FROM MORGANTOWN, IND.

"Greetings from Morgantown." Postmarked 1916.

Water Works, Mt. Vernon, Ind.

The waterworks plant at Mount Vernon, completed in 1886, was a source of local pride in the early 1900s. A hundred years later, the remodeled and expanded building was still being used by the Mount Vernon Water Works Department. Written message: "Dear saster, We are all well and hope you are the same. I am going to have a quilting and wont you to come the 22th of February. Try and get all to getter and come. I have rote to all."

MUNCIE

The seat of Delaware County, Muncie was originally a Native American settlement occupied by Delaware of the Munsee tribe. The area was ceded to the United States in 1818 in accordance with a treaty, and the town was platted in 1827. Known early on as an agricultural trading center, Muncie began to make the transition to an industrial city after the Civil War. Its economy boomed after the discovery in 1886 of natural gas nearby, and it soon became a center for the manufacture of glass and steel. The Ball Brothers Company, which opened there in 1886, went on to be the world's largest manufacturer of glass bottles and jars. Ball State University was opened in 1918.

The Federal Building served as the main post office in Muncie from 1906 to 1960. It later became a convention center. Postmarked 1908. Written message: "Dear Grandparents, We are better. I and the baby have been sick ever sense I wrote you before but are better last week, the first time I ever not got my washing done. I'll send some nice Postals when I get up town. Ma's were all well last Friday. How are all of you, come over when you can would be glad to see you. When have you heard from Robbie tell Eva and Coral they had better ans. my card. It some like winter now. Well come over. From Ethel. Good By."

The First Universalist Church of Muncie was founded in 1859. The original church was extensively remodeled around 1900. It was later renamed the Unitarian Universalist Church of Muncie. Postmarked 1912.

NAPPANEE

The Elkhart County town of Nappanee originated as a station on the Baltimore and Ohio Railroad. It was platted on December 12, 1874, six days after the first train stopped. The original settlers, three Mennonite and Amish Mennonite farmers, laid out fifty lots for the town and donated five acres to the railroad for a depot. They were among the first Amish settlers in Indiana, and Nappanee would eventually be home to one of the largest populations of Old Order Amish in the United States. A number of the town's buildings are on the National Register of Historic Places.

(*top*) The Delaware Hotel in Muncie. Built in 1905, it was the largest hotel in Muncie and was considered one of the best hotels in the state. It was razed in 1970 to make way for an office building. Ca. 1912.

(*bottom*) The Hotel Roberts in Muncie. Opened in 1921, it was designed to be the finest hotel in the city. Later renamed the Radisson Hotel Roberts, it is on the National Register of Historic Places. Postmarked 1934.

East Market Street, Nappanee. Market Street is now part of the Downtown Nappanee Historic District. Ca. 1940.

NASHVILLE

The Brown County seat of Nashville was platted in 1836. A log courthouse and jail were built the next year, on the site of the current courthouse. The country around Brown County was still wild at that time, and the community consisted of about seventy-five settlers in a cluster of log cabins. By the time the town was incorporated in 1872, the area had begun to develop, but Nashville remained a small community until the railroads arrived and made it more accessible. A number of outstanding artists made their way to the county in the early 1900s, including T. C. Steele, and in 1926 the first gallery opened in Nashville, which at the time had a population of only 323. Brown County State Park opened nearby in 1931. The busy town is now a popular tourist destination.

Abe Martin Lodge in Brown County State Park, Nashville. Ca. 1950.

Swimming at Brown County State Park. Ca. 1950.

NEWBURGH

Newburgh is the oldest town in Warrick County. Settled in 1803 by a man named John Sprinkle, it was originally called Sprinklesburgh. From the 1850s to the 1870s, Newburgh prospered as the largest Ohio River port between Cincinnati and New Orleans. It was home to a prominent educational institution, the Delaney Academy, which was founded in 1842. During the Civil War, it became the first town north of the river to be captured by Confederate forces. A traditional Ohio River town, Newburgh has a noted historic district.

Dam number 47 on the Ohio River at Newburgh. Ca. 1940.

NEW CARLISLE

Platted in 1835 and incorporated in 1866, New Carlisle was founded by and named for a traveler and adventurer named Richard Carlisle. The St. Joseph County town began to grow after the arrival of the Lake Shore Railroad in 1852. By 1907 two interurban lines had also been established. The Studebaker Corporation built a proving ground at New Carlisle, where it road-tested cars. The New Carlisle Historic District is on the National Register of Historic Places, as is the Studebaker Clubhouse at Bendix Woods County Park, where pine trees form a "sign" that spells out the name STUDEBAKER.

Michigan Street was the main street in early New Carlisle. Postmarked 1908. Written message: "Dear Frank, Here is our business block. Nice and cooler this morning. L.J.C. Love to Jessie."

471-29

"Dear Frank, Here is our business block.
Nice and cooler this morning.
L.J.C. Love to Jessie."

The Studebaker Proving Ground at New Carlisle. Printed caption: "On this great 800-acre outdoor laboratory . . . facts are separated from opinions. Here every new model—every improvement—must demonstrate its merit in thousands of miles of rigorous testing before being released to the public. Proof positive of the value to you of Studebaker's Million-Dollar Proving Ground lies in the simple fact that Studebaker now holds every official speed and endurance record for stock cars."

NEW CASTLE

The seat of Henry County, New Castle was settled in 1822 and platted in 1823. It began to develop as an industrial city after the gas boom in the 1880s. Maxwell cars were made there from 1904 until 1925. The Maxwell site was later acquired by the Daimler-Chrysler Corporation. Known for products as diverse as roses and auto parts, New Castle is also the home of the Indiana Basketball Hall of Fame and of Chrysler Fieldhouse, which is the largest high school fieldhouse in the world.

First M. E. Church, New Castle, Ind.

The First United Methodist Church in New Castle as it looked ca. 1910, before extensive renovations.

Downtown New Castle ca. 1910. Postmarked 1912.

Broad Street from 14th East, New Castle, Ind.

Chrysler Plant, New Castle, Ind.

New Castle's Chrysler plant produced record numbers of automotive parts in the 1940s and 1950s. Ca. 1940.

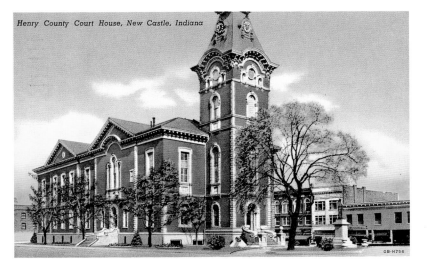

Henry County Court House, New Castle, Indiana

NORTH MANCHESTER

The Wabash County town of North Manchester was founded in 1836. It is situated on the Eel River in northeastern Indiana. The coming of the railroads in 1870 spurred the town's industrial growth. A DeWitt auto factory opened in North Manchester in 1909, producing highwheelers, but it burned down a year later. Manchester College opened in 1889.

Artist's sketch of Manchester College. Ca. 1912. The college used postcards such as this one to solicit contributions for a proposed endowment.

(left) The Henry County Courthouse in New Castle. Along with the surrounding New Castle Historic District, it is on the National Register of Historic Places. Postmarked 1958. Written message: "Dear Winnie; We arrived here this afternoon and had lunch and a good time, so far the dog is healthy, the house has not burned down and Chrysler stock is holding firm. This is the Court House where you should get your Marriage License. 'Lum.'"

ong
may
she
ve!

Greetings from

Bono, Ind.

DIXIE ON LA

Abraham Lincoln's Boyhood

RUSHVILLE
301
LINE

C.F. ALLIS

SOUTH SIDE INN

FURNITURE

South

My dear Nora:-
ibly come th
ut well be a
Friday mor
bect yard t
gage us ro
da & Mary
th be there
be. Mary H
cunning
W. C-1
Ede & Mary are
coming (P.) We w
we were too

CABINS

VORIS & FISHER PRINT

NKLIN COLLEGE

EIGHT

Oakland City to Portland

OAKLAND CITY

Located in Gibson County, Oakland City was platted in 1856. Originally called simply Oakland—supposedly for the groves of oak trees growing on the site—it later added "City" to its name. A post office was established in 1860, and only twenty-five years later Oakland City College (now University) was opened on land that had been donated by Colonel William Cockrum, a Union officer during the Civil War. Cockrum's former home is on the National Register of Historic Places.

Greetings From Oakland City, Ind.

A greetings postcard from Oakland City. Postmarked 1924. Written message: "This is one of the pretty scenes of Oakland City Indiana. We had a dusty drive down here. Virginia."

PENDLETON

Pendleton was named for Thomas Pendleton, who settled in the area in 1823 and platted the town in 1830. It was the seat of Madison County until 1828. The gas boom of the late 1800s brought several glass and tile manufacturers to the town, but a century later Pendleton's largest employers were correctional institutions: the Pendleton Correctional Facility (formerly the Indiana Reformatory), the Correctional Industrial Facility, and the Pendleton Juvenile Correctional Facility.

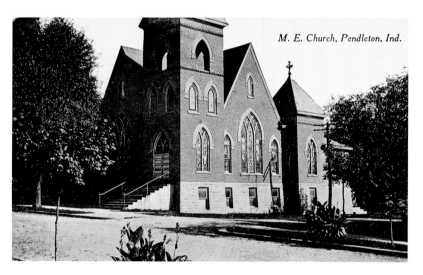

M. E. Church, Pendleton, Ind.

The First United Methodist Church in Pendleton. Postmarked 1918. Written message: "Hello Hazel: Have you completed any more yokes since I left. Best wishes, Ed."

PENNVILLE

Pennville was laid out in 1836. Originally called New Lisbon, the small Jay County town went through a series of name changes over the next few years. In 1836 it became Camden, but there was already a Camden post office in Indiana, so it was renamed Penn, in honor of William Penn and the Quakers who had settled in the area. The Penn post office was established in 1839, but the name changed one final time, to Pennville, in 1840.

"Been going some since Saturday morning touring Indiana. There has been plenty of rain here. How is everything in Ohio. L.B."

School Building, Pennville, Indiana.

Fewer than 500 people lived in Pennville in the early 1900s, but the town boasted an impressive public school. Postmarked 1914. Written message: "Been going some since Saturday morning touring Indiana. There has been plenty of rain here. How is everything in Ohio. L.B."

PERU

Peru, the seat of Miami County, was laid out on the north bank of the Wabash River in 1834, on the site of a Miami Indian village and trading post. The first railroad arrived in 1854, and by the end of the century the town was a significant railroad hub. From the late 1880s until the 1940s, it was also a center for the traveling circus industry. The circuses moved their animals and equipment by rail, and several of them used a 500-acre farm in Peru as their winter quarters, offering plenty of work for local painters, carpenters, woodcarvers, and seamstresses. The old winter quarters later became the home of the International Circus Hall of Fame. It is on the National Register of Historic Places.

The former Peru High School. Postmarked 1915. Written message: "Dear Elva & all: How are you folks? We are all well as usual. Mother is here now, they brought her over Sunday. She seems to be very well contented so far. I have been cleaning house. Wish you could come over. Bessie."

(*top*) Working with the elephants at the winter quarters of the American Circus Corporation in Peru. Ca. 1940.

(*bottom*) The Miami County Courthouse in Peru. Completed in 1910, it was designed in the classical Renaissance style, which had become popular after the World's Columbian Exhibition in Chicago in 1893. Postmarked 1944.

PORTLAND

The city of Portland is the seat of Jay County. It was platted in 1837 and named for Portland, Maine, the home of the man who laid out the town. Originally a farm trade center, it attracted a number of industries after the discovery nearby of natural gas in 1886. Over the years, manufacturers in Portland have produced a range or products, from clothing to canned goods to silos to brooms. The town's old commercial district is on the National Register of Historic Places.

General Shanks School in Portland as it looked in the early 1900s. Built in the 1860s, it was replaced by a new building in 1964. Postmarked 1909.

SOUTH SCHOOL BUILDING
PUBLISHED BY "HALL THE BOOKMAN," PORTLAND, IND.

Dear Ivah:—
The Jay Co Fair begins Aug 20/09 Will be glad to have you visit us again. Dont Know when Co J can come we are talking some of buying this fall if we do we wont by and come now) (Let me know about this) Ione

NINE

Ray to Syracuse

RAY

The Steuben County community of Ray was laid out in 1873. In 1895 it was home to 172 people, at which time it was served by a railroad. By 1930 it had only 9 residents, according to the U.S. census, but by 1950 the population had swelled, to 250. That rate of growth did not continue, however. The post office, which had been established in 1872, was closed in 1967.

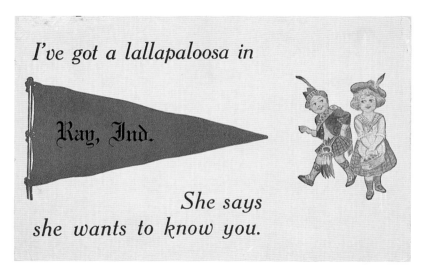

Even some of the smallest towns had their own greetings postcards. Ca. 1910

RICHMOND

Richmond, the seat of Wayne County, is situated on the Whitewater River, just west of the Ohio border. It was settled in 1806 by a group of Quakers from North Carolina who were attracted by its inexpensive, fertile land. The town was incorporated in 1818. In 1881, E. G. Hill and his father began a floral catalog business in the city. It grew into Hills' Floral Products, which was recognized as a leader in the floral industry at the end of the twentieth century. Richmond is home to Earlham College (est. 1859), an independent liberal arts college that grew out of a Quaker boarding school.

The lake at Glen Miller Park, Richmond. The park was named not for musician Glen Miller but for Colonel John Miller, who sold the land to the city in 1885. "Glen" is a reference to the beauty of the setting.

Old National Bridge, White Water River, Richmond, Ind.

MAIN STREET BRIDGE, RICHMOND, IND.

Main Street, Looking West from 9th, Richmond, Indiana

(*top left*) The original Main Street Bridge over the Whitewater River in Richmond. Known as the National Road Bridge, it was built in 1834. It was one of the first covered bridges in Indiana.

(*top right*) The second Main Street Bridge replaced the old covered bridge in 1896. The iron structure deteriorated rapidly because of the unanticipated stress from automobile traffic and interurban cars. Insufficient insulation around the electric wires for the interurbans caused an electrolytic reaction that hastened the rusting process, and the bridge had to be closed in 1914. A temporary bridge was in use until 1921, when the third bridge, built from concrete, was completed. That bridge was demolished in 1998 to make way for yet a fourth span. Ca. 1911.

(*left*) Downtown Richmond, ca. 1940.

POST OFFICE AND MASONIC TEMPLE, RICHMOND, IND.   56219

ROCHESTER

The town of Rochester was laid out on the banks of the Tippecanoe River in 1835 by a local mill owner who had moved to Indiana from the area of Rochester, New York. The Fulton County seat was one of Indiana's leading summer resorts in the early twentieth century. Lake Manitou offered both abundant fishing and first-class hotels. A large federal fish hatchery, built by the WPA, was located on the road leading to the lake. A number of Rochester's buildings are on the National Register of Historic Places, including two round barns. It is the birthplace of Elmo Lincoln, the first movie Tarzan.

(*above*) The Richmond Post Office and Masonic Temple. The former post office is now the home of the Indiana Football Hall of Fame. The Masonic Temple was demolished in the late 1960s. Ca. 1920s.

(*right*) The former federal fish hatchery in Rochester. It closed in 1965, and the grounds became Lakeview Park. Ca. 1950s.

FISH HATCHERY,
ROCHESTER, IND.—6

ROCKPORT

The seat of Spencer County, Rockport was named for the rocky bluffs on which the Ohio River town is located. Rockport was settled in 1808 by James Lankford and his family, who are said to have lived in a cave under one of the bluffs. Other settlers soon joined them, and by 1844 the community was incorporated as a town. In Rockport City Park is the Lincoln Pioneer Village, a memorial to Abraham Lincoln, who grew up in Spencer County and was said to have attended court in this location. Originally a WPA project, it is now on the National Register of Historic Places.

Rising some 200 feet, the steep, rocky bluffs at Rockport offered early settlers a spectacular view of the Ohio River and protection from its floods.

A boat in the Ohio River at Rockport. Dated 1910. Printed caption: "The Event Of The Season. The Big Fair at Rockport, Ind. August 24 to 27, 1910. Twenty-Fourth Annual Fair. Natural Forest. Large Buildings. Plenty of clear, cool, running Water. Members of the I. K. & I. Fair Circuit. The Horse Show is always Fine. The Rockport Fair is noted for its exciting Races. The Most Beautiful Fair Grounds in Indiana. Surely the Best. Certainly the Greatest. Come join in the Frolic."

The Bluffs, Rockport, Ind.

FAST MOTOR BOAT ROCKPORT, IND.

Near Evansville, Boonville, Ind., and Owensboro, Ky.

8A535-N

The Lincoln Pioneer Village in Rockport consists of replicas of log buildings from the Lincoln era, including a law office, a schoolhouse, and a tavern. Ca. 1940s.

ROME CITY

Rome City was platted in 1839. According to local lore, the Noble County town was given its name by Irish laborers who were working on a nearby canal. When they complained about the living conditions in their camp, they were told, "When in Rome, do as the Romans do." Thereafter the workers referred to their meager quarters as "Rome." By the early 1900s, the small community on the west shore of Sylvan Lake was known for its fine fishing. Several elegant hotels catered to the lake's visitors. It was also the site of the Western Chautauqua, a popular event held annually from 1876 to 1906 on Kerr Island. Among the speakers who appeared at the Chautauqua was famed orator William Jennings Bryan. Gene Stratton-Porter moved to Rome City from Geneva in 1913, after the Limberlost swamp was drained. Her home is now part of the Gene Stratton-Porter State Historic Site. The author and her daughter Jeannette are both buried on the grounds.

G. R. & I. DEPOT, ROME CITY, IND.

Old Willow, Rome City, Ind.

(*left*) The Grand Rapids and Indiana Railway Company depot in Rome City. The trains brought in thousands of visitors every summer, both lake tourists and people coming to attend the Western Chautauqua. Postmarked 1913. Written message: "Am having the best time I ever had. Hattie."

(*below*) A romantic lake view from Rome City. This old willow tree was a favorite subject of photographers. Ca. 1909.

KNEIPP SANITARIUM, ROME CITY, INDIANA.

RUSHVILLE

The seat of Rush County, Rushville was laid out in 1822. The county and city were named for Benjamin Rush, a physician, politician, author, and educator who was one of the signers of the Declaration of Independence. Rushville was well served by railroads, and in the early twentieth century it was on an interurban line that made runs to the Traction Terminal in downtown Indianapolis every two hours. The Rushville Commercial Historic District is on the National Register of Historic Places.

(*above*) Kneipp Springs Sanitarium in Rome City. The "Kneipp Water Cure" was purported to have healing properties in the treatment of rheumatism and paraplegia. The building later became a sports complex. Postmarked 1931. Written message: "Dear Calvin— Leaving here today, going back to Ft. Wayne. Do not write until you hear from me again. Sincerely, W."

(*right*) The Rushville Line interurban.

Graham School, Rushville, Ind.

Graham School, shown here in the 1920s, served for many years as the high school in Rushville. After a new high school was built in the 1950s, the old building housed both the elementary and the junior high schools. It was razed in the 1990s.

The Rushville Public Library opened in 1931. Postmarked 1941. Written message: "Kathy, Received draft papers yesterday. Drop me a line. John."

*"Dear Calvin—
Leaving here today,
going back to Ft. Wayne.
Do not write until you hear
from me again.
Sincerely, W."*

SALEM

The Washington County seat of Salem was laid out in 1814. The next year an Indiana Territory post office was established in the town. In 1863, it was among the communities captured by John Hunt Morgan and his Confederate Raiders. Salem is the birthplace of author and diplomat John Hay. Its Downtown Historic District is on the National Register of Historic Places

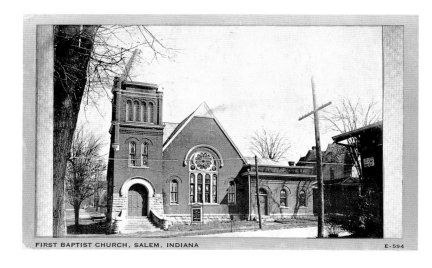

FIRST BAPTIST CHURCH, SALEM, INDIANA
E-594

First Baptist Church in Salem. The building was dedicated in 1901. Ca. 1940.

SANTA CLAUS

The town of Santa Claus was initially called Santa Fe. When its post office was established, the town had to change its name because there already was a Santa Fe post office in the state. Although the exact origin of the new name is unknown, the change was a good move for the Spencer County town. In 1950 the town had a population of only 250, but the theme park Santa Claus Land (later Holiday World) was already drawing visitors year-round. Each December the town's post office receives tons of mail to be marked with the Santa Claus cancellation stamp and remailed.

View of Santa Claus Statue and Main Lodge, Santa Claus Land
Santa Claus, Indiana

The first Santa statue at Santa Claus Land. It was replaced with a different statue in the 1970s. Ca. 1950. Printed caption: "The Santa Claus Statue in front of the Main Lodge greets you with a cherry 'hello' as you enter the park."

SCOTTSBURG

The seat of Scott County, Scottsburg was laid out in 1871. Five miles south is the Pigeon Roost State Historic Site, which commemorates the first conflict in the Indian Territory during the War of 1812. Twenty-four people, including sixteen children, were killed in the attack by a group of Native American warriors demonstrating support for the British. A monument stands at the site of the mass graves.

The Scott County Courthouse in Scottsburg. The simple brick building was renovated in 1997. Ca 1950.

Redman's Cafe, Scottsburg. Ca. 1950s. Printed caption: "Sea Foods—Steaks. Open 7 A.M. 'til 12 Midnight. Closed all day Monday. Specialty—Home Made Cheese Cake."

REDMAN'S CAFE
U. S. Highway 31
Scottsburg, Ind.

SEYMOUR

Located in Jackson County, Seymour owes its commercial success to Captain Meedy W. Shields, who in 1852 arranged to have a new east–west railroad run through his farm, where it would intersect with a north–south railroad already in operation. Later, as a state senator, Shields promoted a bill that required trains to stop at all railroad intersections—including the new town of Seymour, which had been established at the intersection on his farm. The Muscatatuck National Wildlife Refuge opened near Seymour in 1966.

The old high school in Seymour. It was later used as a junior high but was torn down in the 1990s. The stone archway was saved and is still standing on Walnut Street. Postmarked 1921. Written message: "Dear Chum: I guess you have been waiting for a word from me but I didn't have time to write. Every thing is going well & I am having a good time. I have a fine school as you can judge from this picture. Ans. soon Louise."

SHELBYVILLE

Shelbyville was platted in 1822. It is the seat of Shelby County, which was named for Isaac Shelby, a pioneer and soldier who served in both the American Revolution and the War of 1812. In the late 1800s and early 1900s, Shelbyville was a major center for the furniture industry. It was the home of author Charles Major. Major may have been best known nationally for the book *When Knighthood Was in Flower*, but Hoosiers are probably more familiar with *The Bears of Blue River*. On the town's public square stands a statue of that book's main character, Balser Brent, holding two bear cubs; it was moved there from its original location outside Charles Major School.

The Shelby County Courthouse in Shelbyville was built during the Depression with the help of a WPA grant from the federal government. Postmarked 1951. Written message: "Having a good time in the state of Ind. Good place to visit. Vernon."

SOUTH BEND

The site of what is now the city of South Bend in St. Joseph County was once a Miami Indian village and then a French mission. Alexis Coquillard established a fur-trading post on the site in 1823, which soon came to be known as South Bend because of its location on the "great bend" where the St. Joseph River turns northward. A leading industrial center, the city was home to the Studebaker Corporation, which was the only Indiana auto maker to mass-produce cars. The company sold 22,555 cars in 1910, its first year, and 114,000 in 1913. During World War II it built army trucks and engines for B-17 bombers. Other major employers in the early years were Singer Manufacturing, the Bendix Corporation, the South Bend Bait Company, and the Oliver Chilled Plow Works. The University of Notre Dame and St. Mary's College are located in the South Bend suburb of Notre Dame.

The Oliver Hotel, at the northwest corner of Main and Washington streets in South Bend. At the time the Oliver opened in 1899, it was one of the finest hotels in Indiana. After it was torn down, the City Center Building and a Holiday Inn were built on the site. Postmarked 1906.

The courthouse square in South Bend ca. the 1920s.

Oliver Hotel, South Bend. Ind.

Chas.

COURT HOUSE, SOUTH BEND, IND.

11438

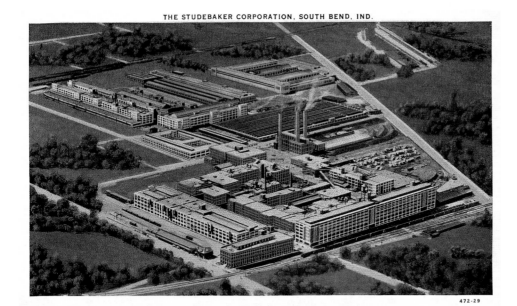

THE STUDEBAKER CORPORATION, SOUTH BEND, IND.

472-29

SPENCER

The Owen County seat of Spencer was founded in 1820. It was named for Captain Spier Spencer, who was killed at the Battle of Tippecanoe. In 1920 it marked the exact center of population in the United States. It is the birthplace of poet and playwright William Vaughn Moody. McCormick's Creek Park, Indiana's first state park, was opened nearby in 1916. The old Spencer Fire Station–Town Hall building (1898) and the Owen County Courthouse (1911) are on the National Register of Historic Places.

(*above*) The Studebaker Corporation grew out of a blacksmith shop and wagon-building business that was started in South Bend in 1852 by the Studebaker Brothers. Printed caption: "Aeroplane view of Studebaker's great One-Profit plants in South Bend, Ind. Studebaker's low One-Profit prices are due to its vast resources, including $105,000,000 in actual net assets. . . . Savings through One-Profit facilities permit the use of finer materials and precision workmanship, resulting in long life built into every Studebaker and Erskine car."

(*right*) The south side of Spencer's town square. Ca. 1920s.

South Side Square, Spencer, Ind.

SWIMMING POOL, McCORMICK CREEK STATE PARK, SPENCER, IND.   F-452

SYRACUSE

The town of Syracuse was laid out in 1837. When the Baltimore and Ohio Railroad arrived in 1873, the community began to thrive, and in 1875 the town was officially incorporated. Located in the northern part of Kosciusko County, which has more than 100 lakes, Syracuse has long been known as a resort area.

(*above*) Swimming pool at McCormick's Creek State Park, Spencer. Ca. 1940.

(*right*) A greetings postcard from Syracuse. Postmarked 1936. Written message: "Dear Mary, I can go to Evansville on Friday if you can. I called the Greyhound this a.m. Only bus is one leaving at 10.25 a.m. arriving at 2.25 p.m. Leave Evansville at 4.30 p.m. Home at: 8.30 p.m. That is to New Albany at 8.30. Fare $3.45 round trip. I wish we could start earlier than 10.25 a.m. Haven't called about trains, have you? Sincerely, Ethel."

In the "Good Old Winter Time"

Greetings from Syracuse, Ind.

TEN

Greetings from INDIANA

Tampico to Vincennes

TAMPICO

The Jackson County town of Tampico, on the Muscatatuck River, was founded around 1840 when a blacksmith set up shop there. It is so small that it is often omitted from state maps. By 1950 it had a population of only 200. Yet in the late 1920s and early 1930s it was able to field some high school basketball teams of county championship caliber. By the end of the century, most visitors to the town came to use the local boat ramp or to attend the annual Grassy Fork Tractor Pull.

TELL CITY

Tell City was settled by Swiss immigrants in 1857. It was named for William Tell, the national folk hero of Switzerland. Situated on the Ohio River, the Perry County seat lies at the far southern edge of the state. Before the arrival of the railroads, it was an important river port.

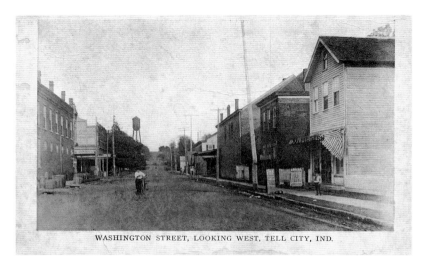

WASHINGTON STREET, LOOKING WEST, TELL CITY, IND.

Tell City's Washington Street as it looked ca. the 1920s.

The Tampico High School basketball team. Ca. 1920s.

TERRE HAUTE

The Vigo County seat of Terre Haute, on the east bank of the Wabash River, was a French settlement from 1720 to 1763. It was dubbed Terre Haute—"High Land"—by French explorers for its location on a plateau above the river. Fort Harrison opened at the site in 1811, and in 1816 the town was platted. As a transportation hub served by the National Road, the Wabash and Erie Canal, and several railroads and interurbans, Terre Haute grew into a prosperous commercial and manufacturing center. Until Prohibition it was also a major whiskey and distillery center. Acclaimed author Theodore Dreiser was born in the city, as was labor leader Eugene V. Debs, who ran for president on the Socialist ticket in five national elections. The first college to be founded was Saint Mary-of-the-Woods, in 1840. The Indiana State Normal School, founded in the city in 1865, developed into what is now known as Indiana State University. Rose Polytechnic Institute, now Rose-Hulman Institute of Technology, was founded in 1874.

First Congregational Church, Terre Haute, Ind.

First Congregational Church in Terre Haute. Postmarked 1910.

Entrance to Highland Lawn. Terre Haute, Ind.

All enter here feet first

13581. Wabash River Bridge, Terre Haute, Ind.

Highland Lawn Cemetery in Terre Haute is the burial place of Eugene V. Debs. Postmarked 1910.

The Wabash River Bridge, Terre Haute. Dedicated in 1905, it was replaced by "twin bridges" in the 1990s. Postmarked 1916. Written message: "Dear Nora:— Arrived in T. H. yesterday afternoon, am going to work in different place. Will give you my address next time I write, as soon as I get time to write a letter. The boss has bought new shop. I am going to run it for him so you see I am getting to be quite important. Hope you are having a swell time going to the revival. Bruno."

"Dear Nora:— Arrived in T. H. yesterday afternoon, am going to work in different place. Will give you my address next time I write, as soon as I get time to write a letter. The boss has bought new shop. I am going to run it for him so you see I am getting to be quite important. Hope you are having a swell time going to the revival. Bruno."

The former waterworks plant in Terre Haute. Postmarked 1918. Written message: "Hello Ethel:— Will fulfill my promise. I have plenty of work down here. I didn't get to see any of the boys at Camp Taylor but Bill Masters and Perry. 635 N. 6th St. Adah. Terre Haute."

The Indois Hotel, Terre Haute. Ca. late 1920s. Built in 1820, the Indois was known by a number of names over the years, including the St. Clair House, the Wabash Avenue Hotel, and the Stag Hotel. It was remodeled in 1928, at which time it was given its final name. It was demolished in 1969.

"Hello Ethel:—
Will fulfill my promise. I
have plenty of work down
here. I didn't get to see any
of the boys at Camp Taylor
but Bill Masters and Perry.
635 N. 6th St.
Adah. Terre Haute."

WATER WORKS PLANT, TERRE HAUTE, IND.   13555

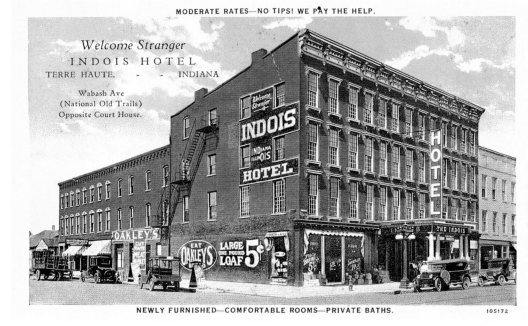

MODERATE RATES—NO TIPS! WE PAY THE HELP.

Welcome Stranger
INDOIS HOTEL
TERRE HAUTE, - - INDIANA

Wabash Ave
(National Old Trails)
Opposite Court House.

NEWLY FURNISHED—COMFORTABLE ROOMS—PRIVATE BATHS.   105172

THORNTOWN

Thorntown, in Boone County, was a fur-trading post in the 1700s. A post office was established there in 1830, and the town was laid out the next year. The name comes from the name of an earlier Indian village at the site, which translates to "Place of Thorns" or "Place of Thorn Trees." The town's first water and sewage system was a gift from Brigadier General Anson Mills, an explorer, surveyor, and Civil War veteran who had been born in Thorntown and was concerned about an epidemic of typhoid fever in the area due to bad water. Despite the arrival of a state highway in the 1940s, Thorntown has remained a small community. The Thorntown Public Library is on the National Register of Historic Places.

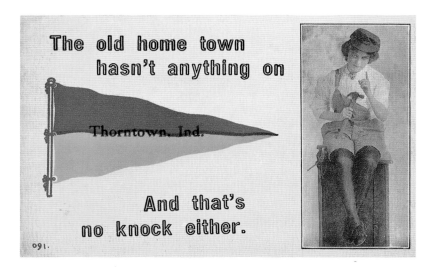

A greetings postcard from Thorntown. Postmarked 1913 via the Chicago and Cincinnati Railroad. Written message: "Hello Eva, How are you? Florence calls you every once in a while. Ethel."

UNION MILLS

Union Mills is a small unincorporated town in La Porte County. The post office established there in 1842 was originally called Bacon, but three years later it was renamed for the Union Mills gristmill, which had opened in 1838. With a few stores and churches and a volunteer fire department, the town maintained its rural character over the years as the population slowly dwindled, from 502 in 1930 to 425 in 1950 to about 400 in 2000. By 2003, however, Union Mills had become a new bedroom community for some of the larger cities in the county.

A horse waits patiently at a hitching post in front of a boot and shoe shop on Main Street in Union Mills. Postmarked 1909. Written message: "Hello: How are you, we are well but Oscar he is sick. We just nearly roast to death it is so hot. What are you all doing. Write soon as you get this, from Norman."

VALPARAISO

The Porter County seat of Valparaiso was laid out in 1836, at which time it was called Portersville. It was renamed the next year for the city of Valparaiso, Chile, where David Porter, for whom the county was named, had fought the British in the War of 1812. Valparaiso University was founded in 1859. Surrounded by lakes, the community is only fifteen miles from Lake Michigan and the Indiana Dunes National Lakeshore. The late "Popcorn King" Orville Redenbacher established his first popcorn plant in Valparaiso.

"Cousin Ella:
Well, here I am in Valpo, Ind. Enjoying
the sights and the beer. Everything is
great and I am feeling fine also. But O
how I wish you were here. . . ."

Looking down Locust Street on the Valparaiso University campus. From left to right: the university chapel (partially shown), the university office building, the pharmacy building, and the medical building. Postmarked 1909. Written message: "Cousin Ella: Well, here I am in Valpo, Ind. Enjoying the sights and the beer. Everything is great and I am feeling fine also. But O how I wish you were here. . . ."

College Place, showing University Buildings, Valparaiso, Ind.

View of Sagers, Valparaiso in the distance.

"Hello Will:
I was glad to get the
picture of the
foot ball team. I would like
to have seen them play.
It is raining here.
Ralph."

❧

View at Flink Lake, Valparaiso, Ind.

(*above*) An early view of Sager's Lake, with Valparaiso in the distance. Postmarked 1909.

(*right*) Flint (not Flink!) Lake, Valparaiso. Postmarked 1911. Written message: "Hello Will: I was glad to get the picture of the foot ball team. I would like to have seen them play. It is raining here. Ralph."

(*above*) Valparaiso University, 1913. Printed caption: "The school is especially well equipped with buildings, apparatus, library, laboratories, etc., for doing the highest grade of work; and whether teachers may have laboratories in their school rooms or not, the fact that they have made their preparation in a laboratory will enable them to present the subject in a much more satisfactory manner than they otherwise could do."

(*right*) Lincolnway in Valparaiso. Post-marked 1951.

VEVAY

The seat of Switzerland County, Vevay was settled by Swiss immigrants in 1802. The post office was established in 1810. Originally known as New Switzerland, Vevay was often called The Vineyard because of its renowned local winemaking industry. The vineyards flourished throughout the nineteenth century but died off after the passage of Prohibition. Vevay is the birthplace of Edward Eggleston, author of *The Hoosier Schoolmaster*. His home and several other buildings in the town, including one of the vineyards, are on the National Register of Historic Places.

An advertising postcard for E. M. Stevens and Company, Vevay. Ca. 1920.

VINCENNES

Vincennes is the oldest continuously inhabited city in the Hoosier state. Situated on the Wabash River, it was initially a French mission. A French fort was built at the site in 1730s. The settlement that grew up around it was ceded to Great Britain in 1763 but was captured in 1779 by the troops of George Rogers Clark. From 1800 to 1813, Vincennes was the capital of the Indiana Territory. The Knox County seat is rich in historic sites, including the George Rogers Clark Memorial, the William Henry Harrison mansion, and the old territorial capitol. It was also the site of the first church in Indiana, St. Francis Xavier, which was established in 1732. Vincennes University was founded in 1801.

The Knox County Courthouse and Soldiers' Monument in Vincennes. Completed in 1876, the limestone courthouse has a different tower at each of its four corners. Ca. 1920.

George Rogers Clark Memorial, Vincennes, Ind. Cost $2,500,000
The Finest National Memorial outside Washington, D. C.

GEORGE ROGERS CLARK
1752—1818

THE CONQUEST OF THE WEST

4B-H796

The George Rogers Clark Memorial in George Rogers Clark Historical Park, Vincennes. Postmarked 1946. Printed caption: "The George Rogers Clark Memorial in Vincennes commemorates the winning of the old Northwest by Col. Clark and his frontiersmen in the war of the American Revolution. Clark and his little heroic army composed of about 170 men captured old Ft. Sackville here and caused the British to surrender on the morning of February 25, 1779, more than two and a half years prior to the surrender of Cornwallis to George Washington at Yorktown. The memorial was erected by the federal government and with the land surrounding involves an expenditure of over $2,500,000. Clark's achievement opened the way west to the Pacific."

The Brock Motel, Vincennes. Ca. 1950s. Printed caption: "Clean, Reasonable and Modern, Air Conditioned, TV, Phones, Garages & Steam Heat for Your Convenience. Ottie Brock, Sr., Owner."

ony may she ve!

Greetings from

Bono, Ind.

DIXIE ON

Abraham Lincoln's Boyhood

RUSHVILLE 301 LINE

C.F. ALLI

SOUTH SIDE INN

FIRST & SON FURNITURE

South

My dear Nora:-

Ede & Mary are coming (P.)

VORIS & FISHER PRINT

ANKLIN COLLEGE

CABINS

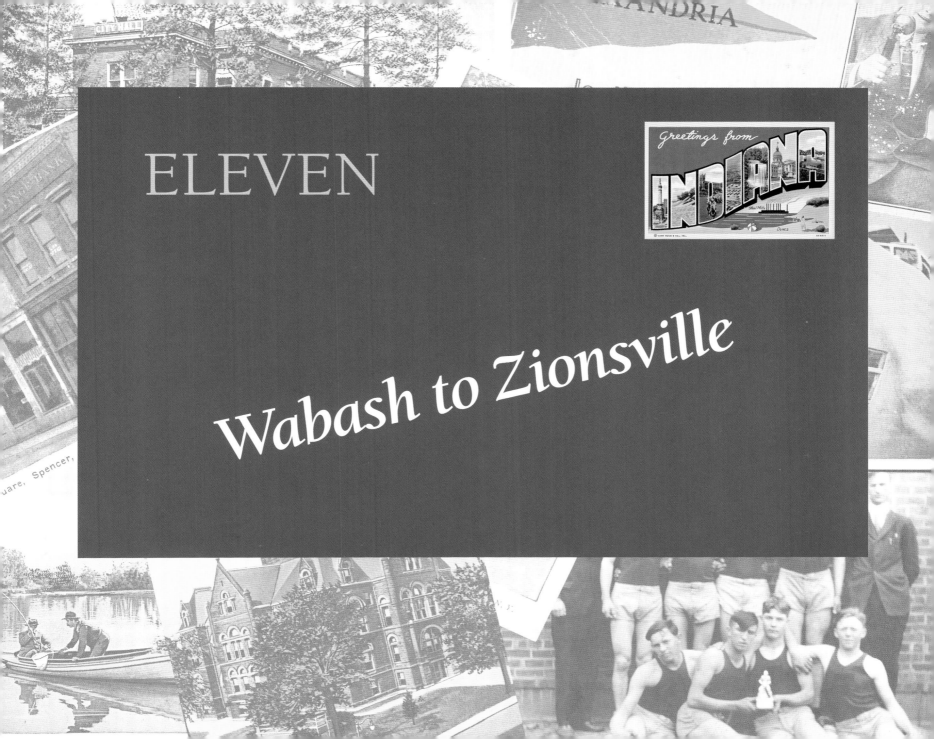

ELEVEN

Greetings from INDIANA

Wabash to Zionsville

WABASH

Wabash was settled in 1827, a year after the Treaty of Paradise Springs was concluded between the Miami and whites. The post office, established in 1829, was initially known as Treaty Grounds, but ten years later it was renamed. The seat of Wabash County, Wabash was incorporated as a city in 1849. Benefiting from its location on the Wabash River, it was a busy port in the early years. After natural gas was discovered in the area in the late 1800s, it quickly developed into a trade and industrial center. It was also the first city in the world with electric lighting. In 1880, four carbon lamps were hung from the courthouse dome to illuminate the downtown area.

(*right*) The Wabash County Courthouse was built in 1840. The minarets were removed in the 1950s. Ca. 1908.

(*opposite top left*) Wabash City Park. Postmarked 1908.

(*opposite bottom left*) Wabash High School. Ca. 1920s.

(*opposite right*) The "Big Four Cut." When this opening was cut through a rock formation near Wabash to allow for the passage of trains, it exposed the remnants of a reef formed more than 400 million years ago, when northern Indiana was covered by shallow warm seas.

Wabash, Indiana. Court House.

CITY PARK, WABASH, IND.

Wabash High School, Wabash, Ind.

3B347-N

Big Four Cut, Wabash, Ind.—3

WALKERTON

Walkerton, located in St. Joseph County, was named for James H. Walker, a La Porte banker, who built the Cincinnati, Peru and Chicago Railroad. The town was platted in 1856. Potato Creek State Park is nearby, as are several lakes. Although the town is small, it does claim a famous native son. It is the birthplace of Harold Clayton Urey, who won the Nobel Prize in Chemistry for his discovery of deuterium.

WARSAW

The city of Warsaw was platted in 1836 and incorporated in 1854. The seat of Kosciusko County, it is situated on the Tippecanoe River. The county has more than a hundred lakes, three of which (Center, Pike, and Winona) are within the corporate limits of Warsaw, and the area has long been a popular tourist destination. The local economy was initially based on agriculture, but as people who came to the area to visit the lakes settled in the city, it soon began to develop industrially. The Warsaw Cut Glass Factory has been in operation since 1877. Zimmer Manufacturing, an orthopedics company, was founded in the 1920s and grew to be a global leader in the industry.

ST. PATRICK'S CHURCH, WALKERTON, INDIANA   N-257

ENTRANCE TO WINONA LAKE, WARSAW, IND.—13

(*opposite left*) St. Patrick's Church, Walkerton. Postmarked 1948.

(*opposite right*) The entrance to Winona Lake in Warsaw. Ca. 1920s.

(*top right*) Warsaw Junior High School. The building was demolished in the late 1980s to make room for the corporate offices of Zimmer Manufacturing. Ca. late 1930s. Printed caption: "This is one of the fine modern schools typical of Warsaw's excellent educational system, well known throughout the midwestern states. Its facilities are well rounded out; each department having equipment and a staff of merit."

(*bottom right*) The Warsaw Armory. This building was in the same block as the former junior high school and was demolished at the same time. Postmarked 1948.

WASHINGTON

Washington is the seat of Daviess County, in the southwestern part of the state. Platted in 1815, it was originally known as Liverpool. The coming of the railroads led to the growth of Washington and had a major effect on its economy. With the arrival of the Mississippi and Ohio Railroad in 1857, settlers began to find their way to the town. In the late 1800s the Mississippi and Ohio set up a group of service and repair shops in Washington, which employed more than 600 people. Construction of the railroad also led to the discovery of large amounts of coal in the area. The railroad economy is a thing of the past in Washington, but coal was still important at the end of the twentieth century, and the area has some of the top-producing agricultural land in the state.

Main Street, Washington. Postmarked 1907.

The City Hall building in Washington. Now part of the Washington Commercial Historic District, it was added to the National Register of Historic Places in 1990.

Main Street, Washington, Ind.

City Hall, Washington, Ind.

114048-N

WAYNETOWN

Originally known as Middletown, the Montgomery County community of Waynetown was platted in 1830. The Waynetown post office was established five years later. The town was named for General "Mad Anthony" Wayne, who commanded the Legion of the United States at the Battle of Fallen Timbers in 1794. Despite the proximity of Interstate 74 and several U.S. and state routes, the town's population remains under 1,000.

The Wayne Hotel, Waynetown. Over the years, the building has been used as a nursing home and for a variety of commercial purposes. Ca. 1910.

WEST BADEN SPRINGS

The Orange County community of West Baden Springs grew up around 770 acres of land purchased in 1851 by Dr. John A. Lane for a health resort. The spring waters were said to cure more than fifty different illnesses, from cancer to alcoholism. The railroads soon made it easy for visitors to get there, and the resort became a Mecca for the rich and famous. The original frame hotel at the site burned down in 1901, and in 1902 the West Baden Springs Hotel was built. With more than 500 rooms, and a center dome 100 feet high and 200 feet in diameter, it was a spectacular sight. The business thrived until the Depression hit. In 1934 the hotel was sold to the Jesuits, who remodeled it into the much less decorative West Baden College. That college closed in 1964, and from 1967 to 1983 the hotel was the Indiana campus of a Michigan business college. The building was declared a National Historic Landmark in 1987, but it sat empty and deteriorating until the Historic Landmarks Foundation of Indiana purchased it in 1996 and set a renovation project in motion.

The north entrance to the West Baden Springs Hotel. Early 1900s.

Bicycle Track, West Baden, Ind.

The double-decker bicycle and pony-cart track at the West Baden Springs Hotel was built in the late 1880s. It was destroyed by a tornado in the late 1920s. Postmarked 1915. Written message: "Dear Cousin: Have not heard from you for some time. I hope you are all well. Mr. Gustafson is drinking the water here and Edyth and I are having a nice trip with him. Regards to all. Lillian."

Rotunda or Atrium of the New West Baden Springs Hotel, West Baden, Ind. Carlsbad of America.

Interior, West Baden College, West Baden Springs, Indiana

78922-N

The atrium of the West Baden Springs Hotel.

The atrium after the hotel became West Baden College. Ca. 1940.

West Baden College, West Baden Springs, Indiana

"*Dear Cousin:*
Have not heard from you for some time.
I hope you are all well. Mr. Gustafson is
drinking the water here and Edyth and I
are having a nice trip with him.
Regards to all. Lillian."

West Baden College, West Baden Springs, Indiana

The entrance to West Baden College, West Baden Springs. Ca. 1940.

(*right*) West Baden College. Ca. 1940.

WINAMAC

The seat of Pulaski County, Winamac was laid out in 1839. Until 1861 it was known as Winnemack, but the spelling was changed in 1861. The town is named for a Potawatomi chief. A small town on the Tippecanoe River, it has long been a popular destination for campers and canoeists.

TIPPECANOE RIVER AT THE PARK, WINAMAC, INDIANA   H-116

The Tippecanoe River at Winamac. Tippecanoe River State Park was established in 1943. Ca. 1940.

WOLCOTTVILLE

Wolcottville, located in Noble County on the Noble–Lagrange County line, was named for an early settler, George Wolcott, who moved to the area in 1839. Wolcott was a busy man who well deserved to have the town named after him. In addition to establishing a gristmill, a sawmill, a carding mill, and a distillery in the town, he built fifteen of its buildings. Unhappy with the local schools, he opened the Wolcottville Seminary in 1852. He later served as the town's second postmaster. Once a center for business and commerce, Wolcottville is a quiet town today.

Before the days of consolidation, all twelve grades in Wolcottville attended school in this building. Postmarked 1908. Written message: "Well girlie how are you and did grandma get home all right I hope so. We are all well and Ione is working. I am just finishing my big ironing. Della has been gone two days. Write me if grandma was all right. Maud."

ZIONSVILLE

The Boone County community of Zionsville was settled around 1830. The town was laid out in 1852 around the newly laid tracks of the Cincinnati, Indianapolis and Lafayette Railroad and was named for the surveyor. It quickly grew, and the town inn was a popular stopping place for travelers. In the late nineteenth century, Zionsville became a cultural center. William Jennings Bryan was among those who appeared at the Zion Park Assembly chautauqua. In the early twentieth century, the town hall was converted to a vaudeville theater and was a regular stop on the circuit. The building is now on the National Register of Historic Places.

"Dear Sir:— Received your letter and am glad to know that you have got a location, and terms to suit your satisfaction, hoping your success, I beg to remain, Yours Respt., Dr. F. G. Brush."

A greetings postcard from Zionsville. Postmarked 1927. Written message: "Dear Sir:— Received your letter and am glad to know that you have got a location, and terms to suit your satisfaction, hoping your success, I beg to remain, Yours Respt., Dr. F. G. Brush."

Greetings from Zionsville, Ind.

Long may she wave!

Greetings from

Bono, Ind.

DIXIE ON

Abraham Lincoln's Boyhood

C. F. ALLIS

SOUTH SIDE INN

South

RUSHVILLE
301
LINE

My dear Nora:-
...ibly come th...
...ut well be a...
Friday mor...
...lect ...
gage his ...
...da & mary...
...th be there
be. Many ...
...inning ...
M C 7
Ede & Mary are
coming (P.) We w...
we were too

VORIS & FISHER PRINT

FRANKLIN COLLEGE

BOBS
CABIN
CABINS

TWELVE

"Wish You Were Here"

The Hoosier state is blessed with a variety of beautiful lakes, a number of which have been popular resort areas over the years. When the railroads came to Indiana in the late nineteenth century, making travel faster and easier, waves of tourists began to make their way to the lakeshores.

Winona Lake, in Kosciusko County, was the site of a general resort as early as the 1890s. In 1894 the property was sold to a leader of the Presbyterian church, who organized the Winona Assembly and Summer School Association and began holding conferences there. Chautauqua programs featured nationally prominent speakers and musicians. Billy Sunday used Winona Lake as his home base, preaching frequently at the Assembly. A number of churches and religious organizations moved their headquarters to the lake, and it became known as a religious resort. At one point the number of visitors was averaging more than 10,000 each summer. The Assembly continued to host summer conferences and programming until the 1980s. In 1994 the deteriorating property was purchased by some local entrepreneurs, who began working to restore it to its former glory.

Lake Wawasee, also in Kosciusko County, is the largest natural lake in Indiana at 3,410 acres. It was a popular summer resort area in the 1920s and 1930s, drawing visitors from within and beyond Indiana. The hotels attracted the rich and famous, offering gambling and musical entertainment by such big-name performers as Glenn Miller and Louis Armstrong. The Wawasee Yacht Club drew crowds to watch the snipe boat races, including the Midwest Regatta. Eli Lilly's family had a summer home on Wawasee when he was growing up, and the lake was a refuge for him throughout his life. It is the subject of his book *Early Wawasee Days*.

Clear Lake, in Steuben County, has long had a reputation as a good sailing lake. By the end of the nineteenth century it was a well-established resort area, offering fine hotels and restaurants, ballroom dancing, and steamboat rides around the lake. On two different occasions in the late 1800s, a steamboat carrying guests from the Hotel Hazenhurst tipped over, killing a number of those on board. By the middle of the twentieth century, the Clear Lake area was a popular family destination, offering a skating rink and a bowling alley in addition to the wide range of water-related activities and active nightlife. Swimmers and sunbathers flocked to the white sand beach on Kasota Island. The hotels and the family attractions are gone now, replaced by condominiums and lakeside homes. The town of Clear Lake was incorporated in 1933.

Lake Shafer was created in 1923, when the Norway Dam was completed north of Monticello, in White County. It quickly became a popular resort area. Ideal Beach was opened in 1926. Rental cottages and a hotel were in operation by the next year, and by 1930 the Monon Railroad was offering weekend excursion trips from Chicago and Indianapolis. The New Ideal Beach Ballroom opened in 1930, and by 1937 it had to be expanded to accommodate the crowds. The 1940s brought a skating rink, a bowling alley, and then a number of amusement park rides. Ideal Beach was renamed Indiana Beach in 1952, and at the century's end it was Indiana's largest amusement park, especially well known for its roller coasters.

Bath House, Winona Lake, Ind.

PUBLISHED BY WATSON BROS.

Feeling fine and dandy, having swell time studying algebra problem that I can't get.

How do you do

Box 865   John.

(*left*) Bath house, Winona Lake. Postmarked 1908. Written message: "Feeling fine and dandy, having swell time studying algebra problems that I <u>can't</u> get. John".

(*below*) Two children enjoy a drink from one of the fountains on the Winona Assembly grounds. Postmarked 1910. Written message: "Well Lolita are you coming this week to see me? John Jasper is going down to his other Grandma's to stay all winter. Then I will be alone. John got in my sugar and got a hand full and then he run and threw it at me. You better come and see us. From your Grandma Hartman."

"Well Lolita are you coming this week to see me? John Jasper is going down to his other Grandma's to stay all winter. Then I will be alone. John got in my sugar and got a hand full and then he run and threw it at me. You better come and see us. From your Grandma Hartman."

402,737   Lilly Pond Fountain, Winona Lake, Ind.

BATHING BEACH, WINONA LAKE, IND.

SNIPE BOAT RACES, SPINK-WAWASEE HOTEL, SYRACUSE, INDIANA

Bathing beach, Winona Lake. Postmarked 1921.

The Spink-Wawasee Hotel on Lake Wawasee, Syracuse. Among its guests over the years were Al Capone, Abbott and Costello, Wendell Willkie, and the king of Siam. After the hotel closed, the building housed a monastery and then a prep school. It was later converted into an apartment complex. Postmarked 1941. Written message: "Dear Dad and Mother, I have been having a very good time. We got here about 12:00 Monday and went swimming in the afternoon and fishing that evening. We will be home Sat. evening. I will be having to close so that I can study for tomorrow. So long. Love Judy."

The Chinese Gardens at the former summer home of Chicago businessman W. E. Long on Lake Wawasee. The traditional Japanese teahouse contained Long's collection of Chinese art. The home was torn down in the 1960s. Postmarked 1941.

The South Shore Inn at Lake Wawasee. It was destroyed in a fire in the 1960s. Postmarked 1941.

"Dear Dad and Mother, I have been having a very good time. We got here about 12:00 Monday and went swimming in the afternoon and fishing that evening. We will be home Sat. evening. I will be having to close so that I can study for tomorrow. So long. Love Judy."

DREAM ISLAND, W. E. LONG ESTATE, LAKE WAWASEE, INDIANA

SOUTH SHORE INN, LAKE WAWASEE, INDIANA

Hotel Hazenhurst, Clear Lake
Fremont, Ind.

The Hotel Hazenhurst was a landmark on Clear Lake as early as the 1850s, known for its ballroom and fine restaurant. In the early years, out-of-town visitors took the train to Ray, Indiana, then traveled on to the hotel in horse-drawn wagons. Postmarked 1942. "Dear Mother: Arrived here yesterday. Very nice place. Good eats. Today it is pretty cool. Paul, Walter and Lowell have gone fishing. Hope they catch some. Hope you are well. We are. There were about 65 last night for dinner. Will write you later. Love Vera."

The Lakeside Hotel at Clear Lake. Originally a large farmhouse, it was built on to over the years and converted into a hotel and restaurant. The building was later used as a summer cottage. Postmarked 1949. Written message: "Dear Eva: I called you and Gene before I left but no go. Having a nice time. We are over to Fremont Ind for groceries and I am waiting in machine too hot on street. We may be gone another wk. Not sure. Love Martha."

C-301—Lakeside Hotel, Clear Lake, Ind.

6 B-660-N

C-321   Mirador Hotel, Clear Lake, Ind.

7B387-N

Shaffer Lake and Dam, at Norway, Ind.   1-nir

The Mirador Hotel was another fine hotel at Clear Lake, with a popular restaurant. It was torn down by the 1970s to make way for houses. Postmarked 1950. Printed caption: "Located on one of Clear Lake's beauty spots, overlooking Kasota Island and the Yacht Club, giving a complete view of the entire lake. The Mirador is the center of aquatic sports and sail boat races, which are held every weekend during the season. Nestled among the trees, the Mirador provides an ideal place for rest and pleasure." Written message: "Dear Eva, Sure swell up here. Every one swell. Nice trip. Martha."

The Norway Dam at Lake Shafer. Postmarked 1926.

*"Dear Eva,
Sure swell up here.
Every one swell.
Nice trip.
Martha."*

Ballroom at — IDEAL BEACH RESORT — Shafer Lake

Indiana's Largest and Most Complete Summer Resort

6897 ó

Roller Rink, Bath House, Toboggan Slide

Ideal Beach Resort, Shafer Lake, Ind.

74731

The Ballroom at Lake Shafer. Postmarked 1948.

Ideal Beach on Lake Shafer. Postmarked 1951.

The paddleboat *Dixie* on Webster Lake in Kosciusko County. Launched in 1929, the sternwheeler was still carrying passengers around the lake more than seventy years later. Postmarked 1940.

The Epworth Forest Hotel at the Epworth Forest Conference Center, a Methodist retreat on Webster Lake. Postmarked 1941.

THE DIXIE ON LAKE WEBSTER, IND.

EPWORTH HOTEL, EPWORTH FOREST, WEBSTER LAKE, NORTH WEBSTER, IND.   C-620

PLEASANT VIEW, CRIPPLE GATE, TIPPECANOE LAKE, IND.

Tippecanoe Lake. Pleasant View and Cripplegate are landings on the lake named by those who developed the area. Postmarked 1925.

Comic greetings from Nyona Lake, near Rochester in Fulton County. Postmarked 1948.

"WHEN ARE YOU COMING OVER TO MY HOUSE?"

REX

286B

Greetings from Nyona Lake, Macy, Ind.

Bibliography

Allen, Frederick Lewis. *The Big Change*. New York: Harper & Brothers Publishers, 1952.

Alsberg, Henry Garfield. *The American Guide: A Source Book and Complete Travel Guide for the United States*. New York: Hastings House, 1949.

Andrist, Ralph K. *American Century: One Hundred Years of Changing Life Styles in America*. New York: American Heritage Press, 1972.

———. *The American Heritage History of the 20's & 30's*. New York: American Heritage Publishing Co., 1970.

Art Guide to Indiana. Bloomington: Indiana Federation of Arts Clubs, Bulletin of Extension Division, Indiana University, 1931.

Baker, Ronald L. *From Needmore to Prosperity: Hoosier Place Names in Folklore and History*. Bloomington: Indiana University Press, 1995.

Baker, Ronald L., and Marvin Carmony. *Indiana Place Names*. Bloomington: Indiana University Press, 1975.

Bird, Caroline. *The Invisible Scar*. New York: David McKay Company, 1966.

Branon, Frederick K. *New World Wonder Atlas: New Census Edition*. Chicago: Geographical Publishing Co., 1942.

Brewer, John M. *Cowin and Whetley's Occupations*. Boston: Ginn and Company, 1916.

Brubacher, Abram Royer. *The Volume Library*. New York: Educators Association, 1930.

Cavinder, Fred D. *The Indiana Book of Records, Firsts, and Fascinating Facts*. Bloomington: Indiana University Press, 1985.

Cohen, Saul Bernard. *The Columbia Gazetteer of North America*. New York: Columbia University Press, 2000.

Collier's World Atlas and Gazetteeer. New York: P. F. Collier & Son, 1953.

Counts, Will, and Jon Dilts. *The Magnificent 92 Indiana Courthouses*. Bloomington: Indiana University Press, 1999.

Dulles, Foster Rhea. *20th Century America*. Boston: Houghton Mifflin Co., 1945.

Flexner, Stuart Berg. *Listening to America: An Illustrated History of Words and Phrases from Our Lively and Splendid Past*. New York: Simon and Schuster, 1982.

Furlong, Patrick J. *Indiana: An Illustrated History*. Northridge, Calif.: Windsor Publications, 1985.

Garner, James W. *Government in the United States, National, State and Local: Indiana Edition*. New York: American Book Company, 1913.

Gitlin, Todd. *The Sixties: Years of Hope, Days of Rage*. New York: Bantam Books, 1987.

Goldston, Robert. *The Great Depression: The United States in the Thirties. Greenwich, Conn.: Fawcett Publications, 1968.

Goulden, Joseph C. *The Best Years, 1945–1950*. New York: Atheneum, 1976.

Hughes, R. O. *Problems of American Democracy*. Boston: Allyn and Bacon, 1922.

Indiana: A Guide to the Hoosier State—Federal Writer's Program, WPA, Indiana. American Guide Series. New York: Oxford University Press, 1941.

Jacobson, Helen, and Florence Mischel. *The First Book of Letter Writing*. New York: Franklin Watts, 1957

Jenkins, Elmer. *Guide to America*. Washington, D.C.: Publix Affairs Press, 1949.

Luxenberg, Stan. *Roadside Empires*. New York: Viking Penguin, 1985.

Manchester, William. *The Glory and the Dream*. Boston: Little, Brown and Company, 1974.

Mariani, John. *America Eats Out*. New York: William Morrow and Company, 1991.

McDowell, Barbara, and Hanna Umlauf. *The Good Housekeeping Woman's Almanac*. New York: Newspaper Enterprise Association, 1977.

Rand McNally World Atlas: Premier Edition. Chicago: Rand McNally and Company, 1936.

Reed, Robert. *Advertising Postcards*. Atglen, Pa.: Schiffer Publishing, 2003.

———. *Greetings from Ohio: Vintage Postcards, 1900–1960's*. Atglen, Pa.: Schiffer Publishing, 2003.

———. *Paper Advertising Collectibles*. Dubuque, Iowa: Antique Trader Books, 1998.

———. *Paper Collectibles*. Radnor, Pa.: Wallace-Homestead Book Company, 1995.

Schroeder, Joseph J., Jr. *The Wonderful World of Automobiles, 1895–1930*. Northfield, Ill.: Digest Books, 1971.

Smith, Lloyd Edward. *New Pictorial Atlas of the World*. Chicago: The Geographical Publishing Co., 1933.

Souvenir Folder, *Greetings from Indiana*. Indianapolis: Morris Brothers Company, 1940.

Stimpson, George. *A Book about a Thousand Things*. New York: Harper & Brothers Publishers, 1946.

Sullivan, Mark. *Our Times: The United States 1900–1925—The Turn of the Century*. New York: Charles Scribner's Sons, 1926.

Taylor, Robert M., Jr., et al. *Indiana: A New Historical Guide*. Indianapolis: Indiana Historical Society, 1989.

Wecter, Dixon. *The Age of the Great Depression, 1929–1941*. New York: Macmillan, 1948.

Weiss, Ann E. *The School on Madison Avenue*. New York: E. P. Dutton, 1980.

Wish, Harvey. *Contemporary America: The National Scene since 1900*. New York: Harper & Brothers Publishers, 1955.

Wilson, Everett B. *Vanishing Americana*. New York: S. S. Barnes and Company, 1961.

Index

Adams County, 49
Alexandria, 2
Allen County, 36–39
Anderson, 2–3
Angola, 4

Bartholomew County, 16–18
Bedford, 5
Blackford County, 57
Bloomington, 6
Bluffton, 7
Bono, xvi
Boone County, 142, 161
Brazil, 8–9
Brown County, xiii, 109

Camp Atterbury, 12–14
Cannelton, 15
Cass County, 90–91
Clark County, 78–81
Clay County, 8–9
Clear Lake, 164, 168, 169
Clinton County, 40
Columbus, 16–18
Converse, 19
Corydon, 19
Crawford County, 95
Crawfordsville, 20–21
Culver, 21–23

Daviess County, 154
Decatur County, 53–55
Delaware County, 107–108
Dubois County, 59
Dyer, 23

Elkhart, 26–27
Elkhart County, 26–27, 50–51,
    108
Elwood, 28–30
Evansville, 31–33

Fairmount, 34
Fort Benjamin Harrison, 34–35
Fort Wayne, 36–39
Frankfort, 40
Franklin, 41–42
French Lick, 42, 43
Fulton County, 124

Gary, 46–48
Geneva, 49
Gentryville, 49
Gibson County, 116
Goshen, 50–51
Grant County, 34, 95–98
Greenfield, 52–53
Greensburg, 53–55

Hammond, 56
Hancock County, 52–53
Hanover, 57
Harrison County, 19
Hartford City, 57
Henry County, 85, 104, 112–113
Highland, 58
Howard County, 86
Huntingburg, 59

Indianapolis, 62–77
Indianapolis Motor Speedway, 62,
    76, 77

Jackson County, 132, 138
Jay County, 117, 119
Jefferson County, 57, 94
Jeffersonville, 78–81
Johnson County, 41–42

Kendallville, 84
Knightstown, 85
Knox County, 146–147
Kokomo, 86
Kosciusko County, 135, 152, 153,
    164, 165–167, 171
Kramer, 87

Lafayette, 88–89
Lake County, 23, 46–48, 56, 58
Lake Shafer, 164, 169–170
Lake Wawasee, 164, 166–167
La Porte, 90, 91
La Porte County, 90, 91, 100–
    103, 142
Lawrence County, 5, 104
Logansport, 90–91

Madison, 94
Madison County, 2, 28–30, 116
Marengo, 95
Marion, 95–98
Marion County, 34–35, 62–77
Marshall, 98
Marshall County, 21–23
Martinsville, 99
Miami County, 19, 118
Michigan City, 100–103
Middletown, 104
Mitchell, 104
Monroe County, 6
Montgomery County, 20–21, 155
Mooresville, 105
Morgan County, 99, 105, 106
Morgantown, 106
Mount Vernon, 106

Mudlavia, 87
Muncie, 107–108

Nappanee, 108
Nashville, xiii, 109
Newburgh, 110
New Carlisle, 110–111
New Castle, 112–113
Noble County, 84, 127–128, 160
North Manchester, 113
Nyona Lake, 172

Oakland City, 116
Orange County, 42, 43, 156–159
Owen County, 134–135

Parke County, 98
Pendleton, 116
Pennville, 117
Perry County, 15, 138
Peru, 118
Porter County, 143–145

Portland, 119
Posey County, 106
Pulaski County, 160

Ray, 122
Richmond, 122–124
Rochester, 124
Rockport, 125–126
Rome City, 127–128
Rush County, 128–129
Rushville, 128–129

Salem, 130
Santa Claus, 130
Scott County, 131
Scottsburg, 131
Seymour, 132
Shelby County, 132
Shelbyville, 132
South Bend, 133–134
Spencer, 134–135
Spencer County, 49, 125–126, 130

St. Joseph County, 110–111, 133–134, 152, 153
Steuben County, 4, 122, 164, 168–169
Switzerland County, 146
Syracuse, 135

Tampico, 138
Tell City, 138
Terre Haute, 139–141
Thorntown, 142
Tippecanoe County, 88–89
Tippecanoe Lake, 172

Union Mills, 142

Valparaiso, 143–145
Vanderburgh County, 31–33
Vevay, 146
Vigo County, 139–141
Vincennes, 146–147

Wabash, 150–151
Wabash County, 113, 150–151
Walkerton, 152, 153
Warren County, 87
Warrick County, 110
Warsaw, 152, 153
Washington, 154
Washington County, 130
Wayne County, 122–124
Waynetown, 155
Webster Lake, 171
Wells County, 7
West Baden Springs, 156–159
White County, 164, 169, 170
Winamac, 160
Winona Lake, 165, 166
Wolcottville, 160

Zionsville, 161

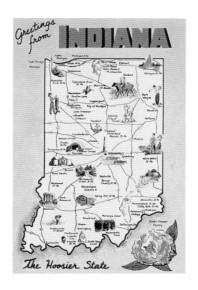

ROBERT REED, a veteran editor of daily and weekly newspapers, has been honored by numerous journalism organizations, including the National Newspaper Association and the Sigma Delta Chi Society of Professional Journalists. His career as a reporter, managing editor, and editor has spanned nearly twenty-five years. He recently published *Night of the Klan: A Reporter's Story,* which documents the Klan in Indiana primarily during the 1960s. Reed has also published six books in the specialized field of antiques and collectibles, and served as editor of the nationally recognized *Antique Week* magazine. He is a graduate of Franklin College and a lifelong resident of Indiana.

Special Project and Research Editor: Jane Lyle

Book and Cover Designer: Sharon L. Sklar

Copy Editor: Jane Lyle

Compositor: Sharon L. Sklar

Typeface: Berkeley

Book and Cover Printer: Four Colour Imports